How to Write for Magazines

How to Write for Magazines: Consumer, Trade, and Web

Charles H. Harrison
Rowan University

Allyn and Bacon

Boston • London • Toronto • Sydney • Tokyo • Singapore

Series Editor: *Molly Taylor*
Editorial Assistant: *Michael Kish*
Marketing Manager: *Mandee Eckersley*
Editorial-Production Service: *Whitney Acres Editorial*
Manufacturing Buyer: *Julie McNeill*
Cover Administrator: *Kristina Mose-Libon*
Electronic Composition: *Omegatype Typography, Inc.*

Library of Congress Cataloging-in-Publication Data

Harrison, Charles Hampton, 1932–
    How to write for magazines : consumer, trade, and web / by Charles H. Harrison.
      p.   cm.
    Includes index.
    ISBN 0-205-31743-X (pbk.)
    1. Journalism—Authorship. 2. Journalism, Commercial. 3. Electronic journals. I. Title.

PN147 .H325 2002
808'.06607—dc21

                            2001046035

Printed in the United States of America

10 9 8 7 6 5 4 3 2 1   06 05 04 03 02 01

CONTENTS

PREFACE

This book began, at least as a desire on my part and then a goal, the day I was told that Myrick Land's thin, blue book *Writing for Magazines* was out of print. You will know how good it was in the classroom when I tell you that students, at the end of the course, actually kept the book. No one sold it! No one gave it away to a fraternity brother or sorority sister who had enrolled in next semester's class. On the last day of class one year, a student, not trying to be critical or smart-alecky, said, "I enjoyed the course, Mr. Harrison, but, honestly, you didn't have to do very much; all we really needed to do was read the textbook."

Believe me, by writing this book I have no intention of replacing either myself or any other teacher of magazine article writing. However, what I have attempted to do is to capture in my book (because I couldn't find Land's equal anywhere else) what students found so helpful in *Writing for Magazines*: a step-by-careful step approach to writing for magazines—a how-to book, if you will.

For example, some texts devote several pages to what has to be the first step in any writing process: Coming up with an idea that you like and that you believe your reader(s) will also find interesting. This book devotes an entire chapter to idea selection. The reason for the added attention is simple. Over the years, I have found that many students have considerable difficulty coming up with an article idea that is worthy of their time and energy and, moreover, worthy of the attention of a magazine editor and her readers. That latter consideration is especially important in my classes, because my undergraduate students are required to query real magazine editors about real articles they also must write and, hopefully but not frequently, sell.

Sometimes students will offer grand, sweeping ideas that could easily translate into *very* long, complex articles. Usually, these students face at least two nearly insurmountable problems that their text and teacher must point out:

- The topic, if it is to be developed properly and fully, will require more research time than there is in an entire semester.
- An editor is not likely to assign to a college student a major article on a topic of major import and perhaps controversy requiring considerable experience and long-practiced skill on the part of the writer.

Another key step in writing for magazines that many texts devote scant attention to is writing the query letter that proposes (sells) your idea to a magazine editor and convinces him that you're the person to write the article. Again, this book devotes an entire chapter to the process. It's that critical. That is, if you want to get published.

Now, here's where I and my book may differ significantly from some other teachers of magazine article writing and other textbooks. Most of the students who come through the course at my university have no intention of becoming a staff writer for a magazine (although some might change their mind later, we hope). However, it is possible for every student to be a freelance writer for magazines regardless of their eventual career field. And at any time in their life! Many professional people wind up at some time writing an article or two (or more) for professional magazines. An auto mechanic and his wife take an especially eventful and eye-opening trip to an exotic land, and he writes an article about the experience for a travel magazine. A CEO for a major corporation helps to conceive and develop a unique and successful business technique that she then writes about for both a business trade publication and an in-flight magazine. The owner of a computer repair business is also an avid fisherman. One summer he experiments with revolutionary new tackle. He has never experienced such great fishing, and he writes about his experience for both a consumer and trade publication.

Every student has the potential for writing for magazines as a freelancer and that is why the chapter on the query letter is so important. I hope you agree.

What also may be a departure from some texts and from some classroom instruction is the attention given here to trade and professional publications and online magazines. I know of two college teachers who have expressed the proverbial two schools of thought on writing for trade and professional magazines. One said teachers of magazine article writing at his institution use a text written by a former member of the faculty that deals solely with writing for consumer magazines. "Quite frankly," he said, "most of my students would not be interested in these outlets [trade and Web publications]." Another teacher reported that he and a number of students who graduate from his course have found work as freelancers and staff writers for trade publications both fulfilling and lucrative. Chapter Eleven points out that a survey of editorial salaries in the summer of 2000 reported that salaries of editors at trade publications are nearly the same as those for comparable positions at consumer magazines.

This textbook is helpful to students and other persons aspiring to write for magazines for two other reasons. First, I write for magazines. I've worked as a staff writer, and I still send in queries to editors, sometimes receive assignments, and sometimes have my ideas rejected. I practice what I preach.

Second, my instruction through the years and, hence, this textbook have profited from the suggestions of students. At the end of each semester, I sit down with students and talk about the course—what worked and what didn't, what was most and least helpful. I have beefed up my instruction and the pages concerning the interview because students told me time and time again how difficult that process is for them. I developed the chart to test article ideas because students said they needed to gauge their ideas against specific criteria. I even included a brief mention of ghost-writing because a student announced in class one day that her gynecologist found out she was enrolled in the course and asked her to help him write an article for a professional magazine.

It is my fervent hope, of course, that you—students who use this book and find it helpful—will keep it on your shelf next to *Elements of Style,* a good writers' handbook, dictionary and thesaurus long after you have completed your course in magazine article writing and have graduated. Myrick Land also would be pleased.

1 Know the Marketplace: Consumer Magazines

Consumer magazines are publications directed at the general public or at special segments of the population, for example, working women, golfers, persons who like to travel, and so on. While news magazines such as *TIME* are intended primarily to inform, and publications such as *People* are designed mostly for entertainment, nearly all consumer magazines serve both functions. An issue of *Reader's Digest*, for example, might include an article telling readers how to lose weight and also a humorous or exciting personal experience story. Most magazines today contain only nonfiction articles, but a few (e.g., *The New Yorker* and *Harper's*) also publish one short story and one or more poems in each issue.

Short stories and essays, the latter frequently debating political and religious issues, were the staples of early magazines. Thomas Paine preached revolution in his *Pennsylvania Magazine,* and, later, John Quincy Adams and Alexander Hamilton were among the famous bylines in right-leaning *The Port Folio,* which espoused the Federalist Party philosophy. The great American anti-slavery novel *Uncle Tom's Cabin* was first serialized in the magazine *National Era.*

Although the short, fiction story is no longer found in most magazines, and highly charged political essays are in short supply, both of those early traditions are alive today as feature articles that sometimes bear the marks of fiction and essays and even how-to articles that address social issues and problems. Just as the short story thrives on plot and characterization, so does the feature article. Just as short stories usually contain a substantial amount of dialogue, so do feature articles, at least in the form of direct quotation.

The feature article was invented in the nineteenth century, when newspaper titans Joseph Pulitzer, William Randolph Hearst and James Gordon Bennett almost simultaneously, but competitively, decided to attract readers with stories about ordinary people doing extraordinary—often bizarre— things. "They [features] were printed entertainment and excitement—the equivalent in newsprint of bombs exploding, bands blaring, firecrackers popping, victims screaming, flags waving, cannons roaring, houris dancing and smoke rising from the singed flesh of executed criminals," wrote W. A. Swanberg in the biography *Citizen Hearst.*

Today, feature articles in newspapers and magazines continue to focus on individuals engaged in exciting, humorous, laudatory and sometimes disgusting activities: the fireman who singlehandedly rescues a family from their burning house, the woman who is retiring as an obstetrician after 40 years and nearly 2,000 deliveries, the crippled boy who just achieved Eagle Scout, the politician who continues to advocate losing causes because of principle, and the serial killer who grew up in luxury but was denied love.

From the beginning, the magazine industry has been volatile, with periodicals coming and going like guests through a popular hotel lobby's revolving door. As early as 1828, the *New York Mirror* made this observation about the still fledgling consumer magazine industry: "These United States are fertile in most things, but in periodicals they are extremely luxuriant. They spring up as fast as mushrooms, in every corner, and like all rapid vegetation, bear the seeds of early decay within them [and die]. This is the fate of hundreds, but hundreds more are found to supply their place, to tread in their steps, and share their destiny." In just the latter half of the 1980s, more than 1,200 consumer magazine were launched, but only a little more than 400 survived into the 1990s.

Specialty Magazines Multiply

This section might also be titled from mass audiences to carefully selected audiences. When newspapers started selling for a penny in the mid-1800s, they were quickly gobbled up by the general populace. The Postal Act of 1879 accomplished something similar for magazine publishers. For the first time they were able to mail periodicals to subscribers at a reduced rate (still true today). As the number of subscribers grew, so did newsstand sales, and before long major magazines such as *Saturday Evening Post* and *Ladies Home Journal* each had a circulation approaching one million. Consumer magazines had become mass media. The *Saturday Evening Post* in particular, and later *Reader's Digest*, *Life, Look* and *Colliers* were general interest magazines. They appealed to men and women of all ages, and they contained articles that suited the tastes and interests of nearly everyone.

After World War II, the marketplace began to change. Television became *the* mass medium, and advertisers in droves spent more and more of their dollars on TV programs and fewer and fewer dollars on magazines and newspapers. Since all magazines depend on advertising to remain solvent, that hurt. Then two things happened, pretty much at the same time. First, magazine publishers discovered they could stay in business or get into the business if they could promise advertisers a hand-picked audience of readers most likely to buy their product. Second, the American people's wants changed. They wanted information and entertainment designed for their particular lifestyle at a particular time in their life.

Here's just one example: Parents of very young children are concerned about a lot of things, but one of them is their child's health and physical fitness. Hence, in 1989, the magazine *Healthy Kids* was established in cooperation with the American Academy of Pediatrics. The bimonthly magazine's carefully researched and technically accurate articles (and, not incidentally, its ads) are aimed at parents of children aged birth to 10 and are dedicated to "the betterment of children's health." Ten years later, according to *Writer's Market 2000,* the magazine's circulation to its specialized audience was more than 1.5 million.

These publications that zero in on a particular readership and offer a limited, carefully selected table of contents are called specialty or niche magazines. Specialty magazines have been around for decades, of course. However, a number of today's specialty magazine categories did not even exist 50 or 25 years ago. *Writer's Market 2000* lists 14 periodicals under the heading Personal Computers. The category was not included in the 1975 book because personal computers were not yet on the market. Indeed, of the 14 magazines listed, the oldest was established in 1982; most began publishing in the 1990s.

Kirsten C. Holm, editor of *Writer's Market,* went back through past editions of that valuable aid to freelance writers and provided the comparative data that show the rapid rise of niche magazines:

Category: Health & Fitness

Year	Number of Magazines listed
1950	0
1975	10
2000	30

Category: Regional (e.g., **Los Angeles Magazine** *and* **Kansas!**)

Year	Number of Magazines listed
1950	0
1975	76
2000	142

Category: Sports

Year	Number of Magazines listed
1950	0
1975	10
2000	30

Category: Travel, Camping and Trailer

Year	Number of Magazines listed
1950	0
1975	21
2000	56

Not only has there been a proliferation of new specialty categories, but many old categories have been divided into a number of sub-specialties. For example, what has happened to the sports category in *Writer's Market*, as noted in the data supplied by Kirsten Holm, offers an excellent illustration of how a specialty category can be splintered into a number of sub-specialties. The current *Writer's Market* lists the number of magazines in each of the following sports sub-specialties: archery and bowhunting (3), baseball (2), basketball (1), bicycling (8), boating (25), golf (11), guns (8), hiking and backpacking (2), hockey (2), horse racing (3), hunting and fishing (41), martial arts (6), motor sports (4), Olympic sports (3), running (2), skiing and snow sports (6), soccer (2), water sports (12), and wrestling (1).

Ladies Home Journal, at 120 years old the matriarch of women's magazines, is still going strong (five million circulation) by providing, according to its editors, a "broader range" of articles than most other women's magazines. But the 300 or so periodicals now competing for women readers have each tried to carve out a slice from the bigger specialty pie. Consequently, subspecialty magazines zero in on women of a certain age (e.g., *More Magazine* for women over 45), income and lifestyle (e.g., *Elle* for the "sophisticated, affluent, well-traveled woman"), even size (*Radiance, the Magazine for Large Women*). Add to the list such periodicals as *Executive Female* for "professional and managerial women;" *Essence*, "the magazine for today's Black woman;" and *Marie Claire*, "with a focus on beauty and fashion."

In 1998, publishers launched 1,067 new magazines, reported Michael J. Wolf and Geoffrey Sands in the July/August 1999 issue of *Brill's Content*. Eight years earlier just 557 hit the newsstands. Today, some 4,500 periodicals are in the marketplace, a 50 percent increase over 1990, according to Wolf and Sands. "The trend is not about to tail off. These new magazines will be tailored to ever more specific audiences, and many will be spinoffs of existing, well-known publications. Already we're seeing magazines such as *People* aggressively use its strong and positive name recognition to launch *In Style, Teen People* and *People en Espanol*."

Matching Contents to Readers

Hendrick Hertzberg's article in the *New Yorker* of July 26, 1999 illustrates how specialty magazines flourish when publishers and advertisers both recognize the value of matching magazine content to a select group of readers. He writes about periodicals for young parents that either reinvented themselves, like *Parents Magazine* (1926), or started from scratch in the late seventies and early eighties "as the baby boomers finally got around to having babies of their own." Hertzberg describes the blessed event in the marketplace as follows:

"Whole new categories of advertisers—not just baby food and toys but cars, beauty products, and insurance—wanted in on the baby boomlet. These magazines turn out to be powerful tools for consumer advertising. Their readers are overwhelmingly new parents, with very young children. These readers are entering a stage of life in which they will be buying a lot more stuff while having a lot less time for comparison shopping. They are by definition receptive; they trustingly put their attention at the disposal of the magazine[s]. . . . No wonder everybody [publishers and advertisers] wants a place at the trough."

It is not uncommon for a company to advertise in several or most of the magazines in a specialty category, because each periodical addresses most of the same subjects. Writes Hertzberg about the magazines honed for young parents: "Their covers are generally the same: a cute, happy baby or toddler against a white background. . . . Their contents are generally the same: cautious, moderate, cheerful guidance on the rearing of small children—most of it recycled, with new details, roughly every eighteen months. Their message is always the same: Not to worry. Sure, there are problems, but you want only the best for your kids. Everything's going to be all right."

Formulas (not babies' as written about in parenting magazines) are what it's all about in the so-called niche magazines. First, each magazine has its own formula, but its table of contents, as Hertzberg pointed out, also may be pretty much the same as other periodicals in that specialty category (but not necessarily for all sub-specialty periodicals in a category).

One specialty category of periodicals that has virtually exploded in the last 25 years is regional magazines. The contents of four such publications for the same month (March, 1999) were examined. Their locales and readership are as diverse as they are widely separated: *Minnesota Monthly, New Mexico Magazine, Pittsburgh,* and *San Francisco.* Each, while unique in some respects, also mirrors the others. Here is the formula that editors, writers and readers for each magazine can count on from issue to issue:

- **Events.** What's doing, when and where
- **Food.** Dining out and local recipes
- **Homes.** Decorating, furnishing
- **People.** Especially noteworthy, interesting men and women
- **Travel.** What to see, where to go

Here is how the formula played out in **Food** for each of the magazines:

- *Minnesota Monthly:* Dining out at a Minneapolis restaurant that "has a flair with straight-up seafood."
- *New Mexico Magazine:* The department *Southwest Flavor* featured "simple Lenten dishes."
- *Pittsburgh:* The department *On the Menu* featured a 60-year-old Italian restaurant.
- *San Francisco:* The magazine highlighted "25 great places where two can eat for less than $25."

Formulas are especially dear to the heart and table of contents of most women's magazines. For example, an examination of the July/August 1999 issues of *Cosmopolitan, New Woman* and *Mademoiselle* revealed, not surprisingly, that each magazine covered pretty much the same ground, albeit in different ways. The formula for each publication includes the following departments: beauty, fashion, health and physical fitness, lifestyle news and tips (e.g., "How to hire a mover," "How getting angry gets better with age," and a feature on how a criminal can "take over your life" if he gets hold of your credit card or ID), and *sex.*

Sex has become a key ingredient in the formulas not only for magazines directed at women and men in their twenties and thirties, but also for periodicals in other specialty categories. For example, teen and young adult magazines. *Seventeen,* a long-established publication aimed at young girls, has jazzed up its contents and is now in the market for articles that focus on "intimate relationships." Then there's the relative newcomer (1997) *JUMP, for Girls Who Dare to Be Real,* which is looking for articles about "quirky, bizarre and outrageous trends," and *'Teen* for girls as young as 12 who are concerned about "drugs, sex and teen pregnancy." Even the aforementioned *Parents* and *Parenting* magazines are conscious of the trend. Stuck in among the articles on infant constipation and thumb sucking are those with titles such as "How to have great sex without waking the kids" (*Parents,* May 1999) and "Curve-enhancing jeans" (*Parenting,* May 1999). According to *Brill's Content* (April 1999), "sex or some derivation of the word" appeared 26 times on the 12 covers of *Cosmopolitan* in 1998 and 14 times on the 12 covers of *Glamour* in the same year.

Glamour magazine is an especially glaring example of what's been happening to many magazines, but women's periodicals in particular. Esther Davidowitz, writing in the *Columbia Journalism Review* for May/June 1999, referred to a phenomenon she calls the "Fuller Effect." The reference is to Bonnie Fuller, who became editor of *Glamour* in September 1998. Davidowitz opens her article by describing what *Glamour* was once—BF (before Fuller): It "has won more awards, including two National Magazine Awards, than any other women's magazine. *Glamour* published big, serious features. *Glamour* ran thoughtful, provocative essays. *Glamour* even covered Washington . . . and every month, no less, *Glamour* took the lead on social issues, such as abortion and the women's movement."

One of Fuller's first acts as editor was to cut out the Washington coverage and add a horoscope designed to provide "psychic details you need for your love, lust and work life." Bingo! The January 1999 issue of *Glamour,* the first with Fuller in charge, sold more than sixteen percent more copies than the January 1998 issue. Davidowitz asked two rhetorical questions: "Are we about to witness what might be called the Fuller Effect? Is what Fuller and her followers [and her success has been duly noted by the industry] tend to do—more visuals and fewer words, more celebrities and fewer serious articles, more sex and less substance—changing the magazine world?" Her answer, of course, is yes. She goes on to quote several editors of other magazines, who, she wrote, point out that Fuller has demonstrated for all to see (and copy) that what really sells in the marketplace today—especially in magazines aimed at young women and men, is sex. With capitals, S-E-X.

Putting Demographics to Work

How do specialty magazines like *Glamour* go about finding readers who want what they're offering? After all, if you are a publisher trying to find your way in the new world of specialty, or niche magazines, success depends on your particular formula, or table of contents, attracting readers with the right credentials—the correct demographics.

Suppose, for example, you were Circulation Marketing Manager for the popular *Working Mother* magazine (circulation 925,000 in 1999) and were in search of new readers (and what magazine isn't). How would you go about finding working mothers for a direct mail campaign? Roni Stein is the Circulation Marketing Manager for *Working Mother* and she, like most of her sisters and brothers in the magazine industry, goes primarily to list brokers. In the case of *Working Mother,* for example, the brokers can easily merge their list of mothers with their list of female members of the labor force. In addition to supplying names and addresses of potential readers, the brokers also can refine the merged list of working mothers, if desired, according to type of employment (e.g., professional or nonprofessional), age and income.

Many magazine publishers and, more importantly, their advertisers, are looking primarily for upscale readers—people with high incomes, said Stein. Income level of readers is not a key factor for *Working Mother,* she said. "You don't have to be upscale to buy Maybelline or Birdseye green beans." Not one ad for either product was found in a recent issue of her magazine, but the advertisers that were included were a blend of those whose products were intended for use by a mother (e.g., Migraine Ice) and those a mother might buy for her children (e.g., Children's NasalCrom).

Publishers with an eye to demographics have noticed, for example, that the Latino, or Hispanic, population in America is increasing rapidly (the Census Bureau estimates that twenty percent of babies born in the year 2000 will be to an Hispanic woman). Crain Communications Inc. reported in the summer of 1999, "When Jose beats out Joshua as one of the most popular names for a baby boy in several U.S. states, it's time to adjust the marketing plan. And that's just what three publishers in the ultra-competitive parenting category are doing." In July of that year, American Baby Group and Parenting Group each began testing a Spanish-language magazine for new mothers by distributing sample copies to Hispanic mothers in selected hospitals.

By the way, that's one method new magazines—or would-be new magazines—use to discover whether their niche magazine will be well-received (and purchased) by the intended audience. Another method is to talk to a focus group at an early stage of planning and get their reactions. A focus group usually consists of eight to ten persons representative of the target audience who are brought to a small, comfortable conference room where they may be shown sample pages or features and where they will be asked pointed questions about the proposed magazine and its contents.

Suppose a publisher decides to jump feet first (head first may be too chancy) into the marketplace with a new magazine, perhaps a spinoff of an existing one (and spinoffs are decidedly on the increase). The risk is not as great as it seems, according to Alex Kuczynski, writing in *The New York Times* (March 29, 1999). "On an economic level, the cost is usually minimal around start-up time because one editorial staff is doing the work of two magazines. If the [new] magazine does not find a sustainable market, the publisher can explain it away as a special interest publication that it does not intend to revive, and still pocket the one-time revenue."

Going Online

Salon Magazine in San Francisco is credited with being the first professionally-staffed, Internet-based magazine. And *Salon* was launched only five years ago! Today, magazines appear online almost as fast as new recordings jump on the Top 40 list. Most print magazines, even those as venerable as *Ladies Home Journal,* find they have to be online as well as on paper in order to compete in the marketplace and to satisfy readers who can't or won't take the time to browse hundreds of printed pages. "The Web is still in its infancy," wrote Michael Ray Taylor in *Writer's Market 2000.* "So far no one has figured out exactly what message its audience wants. But what has become increasingly clear is that the online audience doesn't want to read traditional magazine articles thrown across a computer screen."

Jennifer Steil is associate editor for articles about online publications at *Folio–The Magazine for Magazine Management.* She says many online versions of magazines are quite different from the print versions found on newsstands or mailed to subscribers. These are the primary characteristics of online versions of print magazines:

- Some articles may appear only online.
- Some articles may be shorter than how they appear in print.
- Articles are often interactive; they encourage immediate reader feedback.

Online versions of print magazines usually promote subscriptions to their print publication. For example, the web site for *Seventeen* magazine offers a few articles, but quickly points out: "The entire printed magazine contains fab stuff you won't find online (hey, we can't give everything away!)."

Of course, some magazines are exclusively online; no print version exists. For example, *FringeGolf* is found only at dot com. Like most online publications, its online message to persons who want to write for the magazine is simple: Don't call or write; contact the magazine via e-mail or fax.

Michael Taylor, who teaches "online and old-fashioned journalism" at Henderson State University in Arkadelphia, Akansas, stated in *Writer's Market 2000:* "Since . . . July 1995, hundreds of magazines have appeared online. Hundreds have vanished. The few long-term survivors have changed their basic outlook and content, on average, every three or four months. This means that any print-based information for specific markets . . . may be out of date by the time you read it." That warning covers these pages as well. However, what is not going to change is that the world of online magazines was created in less than seven years and was pronounced good for readers and men and women looking for staff positions and freelance writing opportunities. And the world of online magazines continues to evolve.

Sizing Up E-Zines

E-zines are cyberspace publications available either online or via e-mail, and they bear almost no resemblance to traditional consumer (or trade) magazines in looks or content. Also, they should not be confused with either the growing number of online versions of traditional print publications or so-called paper zines that are mostly about music and have been around since 1939.

According to the fifth annual Media in Cyberspace Study conducted by Middleburg & Associates, a public relations/marketing firm, the percentage of traditional newspapers and magazines displayed on web sites went from 25 percent in 1995 to 58 percent in 1999. While these web sites for traditional print periodicals have steadily increased, e-zines ("e" for electronic) have blasted off into cyberspace like sparkles from an exploding Roman candle on the Fourth of July. No one is exactly sure how many e-zines there are, but John Labovitz, the recognized dean of e-zines, who keeps track of them about as well as anybody can, estimates that their number now exceeds 300. This is how Labovitz describes the world of e-zines:

"Zine is short for either 'fanzine' or 'magazine,' depending on your point of view. Zines are generally produced by one person or a small group of people, done often for fun or personal reasons, and tend to be irreverent, bizarre, and/or esoteric. Zines . . . generally do not contain advertisements

. . . are not targeted towards a mass audience, and are generally not produced to make a profit." In 1995, Labowitz wrote, "e-zines were usually a few kilobytes of plain text stored in the depths of an FTP server; high style was having a Gopher menu, and the Web was just a rumor of a myth. The number of living e-zines numbered in the low dozens, and nearly all of them were produced using the classic self-publishing method: scam resources from work when no-one's looking."

Running down Labowitz's list of current e-zines is a tour d/etrange: Angst, BastardOperator, Chronicles of Chaos, FunkPress, Noway, Scream-Baby, StuckinTraffic, and ZigZag.

In her recent book *How to Publish a Profitable E-Mag*, Angela Adair-Hoy describes how relatively easy it is for one person to start up his or her own e-zine. No printing press and no highly-paid printers, no expensive papers and inks, no bindery, and no large space in which to house the operation. What the self-publisher needs, she writes, is a computer (duh!), an Internet service provider, e-mail program software, an e-mail account, web site, fax machine for orders, and a merchant account to process credit card orders.

Oh yes, the self-publisher needs a topic or focus for his/her e-zine. "Determine what your e-mag is going to be about," Adair-Hoy advises. "What do you know? What can you see yourself writing about for years to come? You will soon be an expert on your topic, so begin with an idea that you already have a knowledgeable head-start on. Also, be sure your topic provides plenty of ideas for secondary products you can produce and sell. If there is nothing else you can sell to your readers, then your e-mag will not be profitable." Income from the sale of original products by the publisher is roughly equivalent to revenue from advertising in a print magazine.

Adair-Hoy suggests these standard departments for any e-mag:

- Questions from readers/answers from the publisher
- Letters from readers
- An editorial by the publisher
- News about your topic (e.g., an e-mag or e-zine about overseas travel would update air fares)
- Feature articles

You will note that, while Labowitz claims most e-zine publishers are not interested in making a profit, Adair-Hoy most definitely is. In addition to urging publishers of e-zines to develop products they can sell, she also advocates that they acquire advertisers. She profiles some successful e-zine publishers in her book. Take Dr. Science, for example. Dr. Science has 17,000 subscribers to his free, daily e-zine (more like a newsletter, which a number of e-zines truly are). He provides "peculiar answers to strange science questions submitted by his readers," writes Adair-Hoy. Dr. Science makes money by selling his Dr. Science

Screen Saver for $7.95, Dr. Science mouse pad for $9.95, Dr. Science tee shirts and sweat shirts starting at $13.95, and a host of other items such as coffee mugs and audio cassettes. In addition to all that, Dr. Science has paid advertising.

The e-zine phenomenon is not without its critics. David Nicholson, writing in the *Washington Post* in January 1996, quotes Soia Broskowitz, then editor and publisher of *Omnivore* magazine: "In a print [magazine], the reader doesn't see the not-so-good stuff that was submitted and rejected. But when a [zine], be it paper or electronic, is operating in the style of an anthology of Who's Submitting rather than Who's Blowing the Reader Away With Outstanding Work, then, well, garbage in, garbage out." Nicholson agrees with Broskowitz, at least in part: "It's true [that zines contain some garbage] as looking at even a cursory selection of the e-zines on Labowitz's list will show. . . . Still, if sampling the e-zines can be frustrating, it can be exhilarating as well, sort of like a town meeting."

Go Figure Formulas

The content of magazines, both print and online, is usually organized according to a formula. The formulas of magazines may be identified by the titles of their article categories and departments. For example, such headings as *profile, latest news, entertainment, dining out, fashion,* etc.

Speaking of formulas, if you haven't noticed already, glance through a batch of magazines and spot how many titles of articles in departments and features contain or imply the words "how to."

- How to manage money
- How to build or repair something
- How to travel without spending a lot of money
- How to improve your sex life
- How to cope with depression
- How to survive a broken relationship
And so on.

How-to articles (how-to books also are very popular) are often based on the writer's personal experience and expertise or on the knowledge and work of persons familiar to the writer.

Know Your Audience

Magazine publishers employ demographics and list brokers to identify a readership for their publication. The publisher trying to establish a niche in the world of consumer magazines has spent considerable time defining and refining the audience for his or her specialty publication. The format and formulas probably have been pretested with focus panels or through sampling to determine reactions and opinions of the carefully selected audience. Readers may have been selected according to some or all of the following criteria: age, education, gender, geographical location, income, lifestyle, occupation, race, and religion.

Here's how you get to know an audience—a magazine's readers—in advance so that you know how to write articles in the correct style and tone for that audience:

Read the magazine for which you hope to write. Editors say they are constantly amazed, frustrated and disheartened by the number of writers who submit material that is obviously unsuited for their readers. For example: the editor of a juvenile magazine aimed at children aged 7–12 receives an article about teenage dating; the editor of a Midwest regional magazine rejects an article about the Pine Barrens of New Jersey; a woman who has written about her battle with depression is turned down because the magazine to which she submitted the piece caters to sophisticated, highly educated readers who buy the magazine because of its scholarly and authoritative articles about mental illness.

Analyze the writing and advertisements. They tell much about the readers. If one were to compare *Parade* magazine with the *New Yorker,* for example, most differences between the two would be immediately noticeable. *Parade,* like many publications aimed at a mass readership of both sexes roughly between the ages of 25 and 40, offers a number of short, glitzy features on entertainment celebrities. The *New Yorker* also may have features on personalities, but they are written for a more mature, better educated reader who leans toward in-depth profiles about political and business leaders or arts virtuosos.

If you were to apply a readability formula to the writing in the two publications, you would find that most articles in *Parade* score six to eight whereas articles in the *New Yorker* are most likely to score in the neighborhood of ten to twelve. Robert Gunning, whose Fog Index is one readability formula, equates the scores with reading level. The majority of Americans are most comfortable reading at a level of nine or below.

The Gunning Fog Index works this way:

- Select a passage of approximately 100 words (a few words either side will not be a factor).
- Determine the average sentence length of the passage. If the passage contained six sentences of 22, 19, 11, 18, 20 and 10 words respectively, the average length would be approximately 17 (100 divided by six).

- Count the number of words in the sample that contain three or more syllables. However, do not count proper nouns and verbs whose -ed or -es ending creates the third syllable (e.g., decided).
- Add the average sentence length and number of words of three syllables or more and multiply by 0.4.

If average sentence length is 15, and the passage contains only two words of three syllables or more, the score would be six.

The score of the passage in the *New Yorker* article was increased by words such as "aesthetic" and "cognizant," words not likely to appear in a *Parade* article.

You should also scan advertisements. An issue of *Parade* featured an ad for audio cassettes ("Greatest Italian Love Songs") and one for a paperback book club. On the other hand, an issue of *The New Yorker* contained an ad for a fine art catalog and several ads promoting travel to the Caribbean and Europe. There is no question whose readers would be classified as upscale.

Read what editors have to say about their magazine. A reference work like *Writer's Market* contains tips from editors. Read them. Here are some examples from *Writer's Market 1999*:

"Read the journal and assess the range of contents and the level of writing." *Michigan Quarterly Review*

"Bimonthly magazine . . . for people who are well-educated, activist, outdoor-oriented and politically well-informed with a dedication to conservation." *Sierra*

"Use an informal easy-to-read style rather than a philosophical, academic tone." *Christian Home and School*

"Tailored for young women in their teens and early twenties. Writers have to ask themselves whether or not they feel they can find the right tone . . . a tone which is emphatic yet never patronizing; lively yet not superficial." *Seventeen*

"Articles should be directed at a national audience. Our readers are warm and loving. They want to read about others with heart. Send us something that will make us cry with joy." *Grit*

FOR EXAMPLE

The contents from the November 2000 issue of *Traditional Home* magazine that follow (Figures 1.1 and 1.2) illustrate how a magazine's formula, categories, and departments help inform what kinds of articles the editors and the magazine's readers are looking for.

You can tell something about a magazine's audience by the readability level of the writing. Here are writing samples from *Harper's* and *New Woman*,

T R A D I T I O N A L   H O M E™

230 COVER STORY

261

C O N T E N T S

VOLUME XI ISSUE V

128

74

Continued on page 16

COVER PHOTOGRAPH: JON JENSEN

FIGURE 1.1

Reprinted by permission of Meredith Corporation.

C O N T E N T S

Traditional Home®, November 2000 issue. Traditional Home is
published by the Publishing Group of Meredith Corp., 1716 Locust
St., Des Moines, IA 50309-3023. © COPYRIGHT MEREDITH
CORPORATION 2000. ALL RIGHTS RESERVED. PRINTED IN U.S.A.

FIGURE 1.2

Reprinted by permission of Meredith Corporation.

magazines. Of course, they differ in audience and content in some very obvious ways. But the readability level also tells something about their audience—something a freelance writer needs to know. Following are writing samples from each magazine. Each sample is from the lead paragraphs of a cover story and each contains a little more than 100 words.

"Wheaties" by Shane DuBow (Harper's, August 1999)
"Out of grain-belt towns where pickups outnumber people, and meager rains mean meager yields, and every census since 1920 has recorded more farms lost forever to bank foreclosures and to the depopulating tug of urban jobs, the custom cutters appear each spring on Great Plains highways, with their cell phones and semi rigs, towed combines and towed grain bins, fax-equipped mobile homes and file folders packed with unpaid bills. Soft-stomached, strong-armed men motoring south toward the climes where the crops ripen first. At truck stops from Moose Jaw Saskatchewan, to Shackleford County, Texas, they stop for sweet tea and high-noon 'dinners,' their orders full of yes ma'ams and well-done meats." (109 words)

"How to Stay Close to the People You Love" by Rebecca Barry (New Woman, July 1999)
"About a month ago my friend Sharon called to tell me that her marriage was over. She was fine, she said, but didn't have much energy to talk about it. She'd moved out, and she didn't want me to worry in case I tried her at her old number. I got off the phone and sat still for a long time. Sharon and I have been friends for almost 10 years. We've shared apartments and vacations. I was a bridesmaid at her wedding, and it was to her house that I retreated after my longest love affair fell apart. More recently, we'd drifted." (103 words)

The sample from *Harper's* has an average sentence length of 36, thanks primarily to the opening sentence. It has six words of three syllables or more. Using the Gunning Fog Index, add the average sentence length and the number of words with three syllables or more and multiply by 0.4. The score is almost 17. That score, roughly equivalent to a reading level, is probably three to five points above the average score for the magazine, but, regardless, one could safely conclude that most readers of *Harper's* are highly sophisticated and college-educated. The tone is formal, authoritative.

The sample from *New Woman* has an average sentence length of 12 (only one of eight sentences over 20 words). It has four words of three syllables or more. Again using the Gunning Fog Index, calculate a score of 6.4. This may be a couple of points lower than the average for the magazine. However, the score indicates that *New Woman* is aimed at an audience that is less sophisticated than the audience for *Harper's* and may include a number of persons with less than a college education. The tone is informal, conversational.

HANDS ON

1. Examine the table of contents—the formula—for two or three magazines in different specialties (e.g., *Parents, Natural History* and *Esquire*). What kinds of topics are of most interest to readers? Notice the number of how-to articles.

   - Using the same magazines, notice the tone of the writing. Is it conversational, even breezy? Are slang terms used? Is the tone more formal, sophisticated?

   - Again using the same magazines, apply the Gunning Fog Index to each. What do the scores tell you about audience?

   - Find the listing for each magazine in *Writer's Market.* Read what the editor has to say about content, audience and tone.

2. Explore the world of e-zines. Here are a couple of titles you might take a look at: *L.A. Woman Magazine, Resonance–A Cynic's Guide to Modern Life,* and *S & B Music-SynthePunk Magazine.*

3. Using newspaper and periodical library databases, find one article published within the past six months that describes some trend or important development in the ever-changing world of consumer magazines.

2 Know the Marketplace: Trade Magazines and Professional Journals

The first words to describe the marketplace for trade magazines and professional journals are *big, huge, gargantuan,* and any other synonym you can find in *Roget's Thesaurus.*

James E. Gruning and Todd Hunt, in their book *Managing Public Relations,* give you an idea as to how extensive the world of trade publications is: "Today, almost every company and organization publishes at least one newsletter or magazine, and some have as many as a dozen aimed at various internal and external audiences. Industrial publications, company publications, and 'the business press' are terms usually associated with vehicles packaged primarily for external audiences. Trade publications are aimed at segments of the professionals in a specific area of manufacturing or service. . . ."

At least 5,000 trade publications are listed by the American Business Press, according to Marie Fowler, manager of educational services. The *Encyclopedia of Business Information Sources* lists thousands of periodicals and newsletters for business and industry under 1,200 topics, or headings, from Abrasives Industry to Zinc Industry. The heading Banks and Banking alone (and there are several topics related to banking) includes five weekly newsletters; nine monthly magazines, journals and newsletters; and a half dozen other publications issued bimonthly or quarterly.

And then there are the association publications. The American Society of Association Executives boasts 25,000 member professional associations, and nearly all of them publish a newsletter or journal or both. The *Encyclopedia of Associations* contains 23,000 organizations. The book lists 18 kinds of organizations, including trade and business, governmental, educational and cultural, religious, athletic and sports, chambers of commerce, and labor unions, even fan clubs.

SLACK Incorporated in Thorofare, New Jersey, provides an excellent example of what's happening with professional publications today. It is one of the major publishers in the health care field, producing some 30 journals and news magazines. At the start, it is important to know the difference between a professional journal and professional news magazine. A journal is devoted almost exclusively to articles about the latest research; the authoritative articles are written by professionals and are reviewed by other professionals in the field (peer review). A news magazine, on the other hand, includes articles reporting recent developments in the profession and also general information important to professionals.

SLACK publishes *Orthopedics* and *Orthopedics Today*. The journal *Orthopedics* is described as a "prestigious scientific journal" offering "original, peer-reviewed articles [covering] the entire spectrum of orthopedic surgery and treatment." The news magazine *Orthopedics Today* reports "the latest clinical advances" but also "socioeconomic news related to the practice of orthopedics."

Many magazine writers, particularly those just starting out, know only consumer publications (and often just a select few of them) and are unaware of trade and professional publications. Or they dismiss these publications out of hand because they believe they must have full familiarity and knowledge of an industry or profession in order to write for their journal, magazine and newsletter. Not so, for two reasons:

- Professional news magazines and newsletters include much more than articles about recent advances in a particular field. "Physicians are healers, but they're also business persons," said John C. Carter, publisher of the Journal Division at SLACK. Therefore, while they are concerned about the latest procedures and techniques, physicians also want help furnishing their offices and investing their money; they need to be advised how recent legislation and governmental regulations will affect them and/or their patients; and they and their family need information about interesting travel destinations. "We have practice management and business sections in all our news magazines," said Carter.

- Writers for trade and professional publications advise that technical language and insiders' jargon (and every trade and profession has them) can be learned rather quickly simply by asking questions of sources and consulting, as necessary, a dictionary or encyclopedia of terms used in this industry or that profession. Staff writers and freelance writers for SLACK news magazines, for example, are journalists, said Carter, not health care specialists. When SLACK hires a staff writer for one of its news magazines, it provides in-house training that includes an introduction to terminology peculiar to the field about which the writer will be reporting.

Cassandra Richards is managing editor of *Infectious Diseases in Children, The News Source for Today's Pediatrician*. She has no medical background whatsoever, said Carter, but she has spent a number of years on the beat, which includes covering hearings conducted by the Federal Drug Administration and other governmental and professional agencies pertaining to children's diseases and their treatments. In fact, Carter said, she probably knows more about vaccines for childhood diseases than any other journalist, and even some physicians. "She's earned the title Vaccine Queen." You'll hear from Richards and other writers in later chapters.

A number of journals are the official publication of an association. For example, *Journal of Accountancy* is the monthly publication of the American Institute of CPAs and *NEA Today* is published by the National Education Association. Many association journals (and some trade publications) have a controlled circulation. That means the journal goes exclusively or primarily to members of the association as a benefit paid for by dues. In the case of trade publications, the magazine or newsletter may circulate only among those engaged in a particular industry or business. In other instances, the circulation may be mixed: part controlled and part paid. *The Journal of Refractive Surgery* is the official publication of the International Society of Refractive Surgery and is published by SLACK. According to Carter, Society members account for half the circulation, and the remaining half consists of paid subscribers.

Publishing in Both Worlds

It is not uncommon for a publisher to produce publications in one or more specialty areas and in both the consumer and trade/professional marketplaces. *Bacon's Magazine Directory* lists nearly 500 multiple magazine publishers. Some of these publishers have only three or four publications, but a number of them produce more than 50. PRIMEDIA Communications in New York, which has expanded rapidly and greatly since 1998 to become one of the giants in the magazine industry, publishes 200 or more consumer and trade periodicals, including *Bacon's Magazine Directory*. Truthfully, it is often difficult to nail down who owns what, for the reasons that both consumer and trade/professional magazines come and go, oftentimes very quickly, and because large publishing companies sometimes acquire smaller publishers and gather them loosely under one giant umbrella. Take for example Affinity Group, Inc. of Ventura, California, whose special area is travel and camping, with niches or sidelines in snowmobiling, motorcycling and all-terrain vehicle driving. Affinity includes Ehlert Publishing Group in Minnetonka, Minnesota, TL Enterprises in Ventura, and Woodall Publishing Company in Lake Forest, Illinois, under its ever-widening umbrella.

Ehlert publishes three consumer magazines that collectively tell readers pretty much all they need or want to know about snowmobiles (riding, racing, adorning with accessories, maintaining and just plain tinkering): *Snowmobile, Snow Goer* and *Snow Week. Bacon's Magazine Directory* describes *Snowmobile* as a publication "targeted to the snowmobile enthusiast." Its articles "focus on equipment evaluations, mechanical advice, outerwear and fashion, lifestyle issues, as well as personality profiles and travel." *Snow Goer* is aimed at the "hard core" enthusiast who is into adding specialized equipment to his/her snowmobile, and *Snow Week* caters to the snowmobile racer. Ehlert also publishes *Bowhunting World* for those who prefer shooting an arrow through the air over plowing through snow.

TL Enterprises publishes *Trailer Life* and *Motor Home,* monthly magazines which cater to recreation vehicle (RV) owners who are primarily over age 50 and retired. *Roads to Adventure,* an annual in 1999, was introduced to attract the baby boomers buying their first RV. TL Enterprises also puts out *American Rider,* "for today's upscale Harley-Davidson market," and *Rider,* for the "touring and sport touring motorcycle enthusiast with an accent on performance." Affinity Group also publishes consumer magazines for owners of water craft and all-terrain vehicles (ATVs).

As natural complements to its consumer publications, Affinity Group publishes two major trade magazines: *RV Business,* "which caters to a specific audience of people who manufacture, sell, market, insure, finance, service and supply components for recreational vehicles," and *Power Sports Business,* which is aimed primarily at a national network of dealers in—what else— snowmobiles, motorcycles, ATVs and personal water craft.

PRIMEDIA publishes most of its many trade publications under the name Intertec Publishing and primarily in eight areas: agribusiness (e.g., *National Hog Farmer*), communications (e.g., *Global Telephony*), electrical and public services (e.g., *Energy Manager*), entertainment (e.g., *Broadcast Engineering*), industrial (e.g., *Coal Age*), marketing (e.g., *Customer Support Management*), professional services and apparel (e.g., *Textile World*), and transportation (e.g., *Fleet Owner*). PRIMEDIA's 60-plus consumer magazines are published under both McMullen Argus Publishing and PRIMEDIA labels. They include *American Baby, New York, Seventeen* and *Soap Opera Digest;* a number of periodicals devoted to those who delight in working on and racing cars (e.g., *Drag Racing USA*) and regional bridal magazines (e.g., *Houston Bride* and *Michigan Bride*).

In the world of trade publications, keywords are business-to-business, and Cahners Business Information of Newton, Massachusetts boasts it is "the world's largest business-to-business information provider in the United States. Building around core products—our branded publications—we strive to provide the essential must-have information that our readers need. . . ."

Cahners publishes 130 "targeted print magazines." The term "targeted" is similar to the term "controlled" when it comes to circulation. It means the magazine is aimed at specialists working in a specific industry. Cahners' publications cover a wide, diverse range of industries. For example: *Building Design & Construction* (for architects, engineers and construction managers working on *nonresidential* buildings), *Lasers & Optronics* ("the only new-product tabloid to serve the lasers and electro-optics market," *Travel Weekly* (for travel agents and managers of travel agencies), and *Video Business* (for "retailers who sell and rent prerecorded video products").

Publishing Online

The majority of trade/professional journals and magazines are now on the Internet with their own web sites, according to Yaquoi Moore, marketing communications coordinator for American Business Press. However, the primary reason for being online, she said, is to attract new readers to the print version of the publication. Trade and professional publications have web sites to "broaden their reach," and to attract as readers of the magazine people who have first heard about the publication on the web site.

Generally, Moore said, trade/professional periodicals provide information and articles on their web sites that are not available in their printed publications. "They normally don't duplicate what is in their publication." In other words, the web site version of the publication is not necessarily the same as the printed version.

All of SLACK's journals and news magazines, for example, are represented on its web site (www.slackinc). Many of the publications provide abstracts of articles that have appeared in the print versions and some print full texts of articles, but no publication is duplicated in its entirety online. Also, SLACK offers an online service called Medical Matrix. Anyone with a legitimate purpose can register, and a writer is someone with a legitimate purpose (usually). Medical Matrix offers considerable information in an amazing number of categories. For example, 2,664 pieces of information are available in almost 60 subject areas listed as *Specialties,* from AIDS to urology. Under the *Literature* heading of Medical Matrix, the writer-researcher can link up with the prestigious *New England Journal of Medicine* (think of all the stories in the lay press that have come from articles in the NEJM).

John Carter of SLACK refers to the increase in the number of mergers and acquisitions in the magazine industry as "warehousing." Corporations like Affinity, PRIMEDIA and Cahners are buying up smaller publishers, he believes, because "they are uncertain about the future of magazine publishing." A big part of the uncertainty has to do with the question of whether online publishing will go in a direction no one now can predict. Carter, however, cannot imagine that most readers will scroll through entire editions of a magazine or journal. He thinks readers-researchers will continue to use the Internet and magazine web sites to find one or more articles from different publications dealing with a subject in which they are interested.

Moore of American Business Press also does not see online web sites replacing printed publications. For one thing, display advertising, which goes a long way toward paying a magazine's bills, may be more effective in print than online.

An article by Anne M. Russel in the January 1999 edition of *Folio: The Magazine for Magazine Management* describes the complicated goings on involving Cahners and the volatile nature of the magazine industry. (Interestingly, *Folio* is published by PRIMEDIA, so it is one conglomerate writing about another conglomerate.) In September 1997, Cahners acquired one of its competitors, Chilton Publications, for $447 million. But Cahners is itself a unit of another, larger entity, Reed Elsevier, a jointly owned British-Dutch corporation head-quartered in London. To further complicate matters, Russel quotes David Lei-bowitz, managing director at Burnham Securities, as questioning the future relationship between Cahners and its parent company: "Given statements that have been made by the company [Reed Elsevier] . . . I would be very sur-prised if [the sale of Cahners] is not something that has been looked into."

Commenting on overall activity in the magazine industry, Leibowitz is quoted by Russel as saying, "The number of companies joining the fray [as in-formation providers] is monumental. Given the number of media sources and emerging new media sources, one suspects that we will be seeing a shakeout in the near future. Consolidation is already underway."

Does Your Doctor Need a Writer?

The gynecologist who attended a student learned that she was enrolled in a magazine writing class and asked if she would be interested in editing and rewriting, as necessary, an article he was submitting to a professional publi-cation. The student said yes, and he paid her rather well for the assistance. When you examine the market for professional and trade publications, in both areas opportunities exist to assist the professional and business person. John Carter at SLACK said freelance medical writers regularly work with doctors and medical researchers who have articles to submit to journals.

Professionals and business executives are most interested in having their peers learn about their research or other accomplishments (e.g., an innovation that improved plant production). Of course, they know what they want to say in their article, but their expertise may not be in writing. That is where the freelance writer comes in. The article in almost all cases will carry only the by-line of the professional or business executive, but the writer gets to show off his/her skill and add to his/her income.

As a writer, you can't afford to ignore the trade and professional maga-zine marketplace. It's just too huge and diverse. And remember, you don't have to be an expert in any subject to learn what you need to know about it and then write about it. That's one of the great values of a liberal arts or gen-eral education, as my high school English teacher pointed out years ago. When I was thinking of enrolling in a one-year program at a journalism trade school, my teacher said, "If you truly want to be a *good* journalist, go to a four-year, liberal arts college and take something from everything. If nothing else, you will graduate knowing what questions to ask." It's the best advice I've ever been given. I didn't start out knowing a great deal about most of the subjects I've written about over the years, but I wasn't afraid to ask questions, lots of them.

Actually, you might be surprised at how much you already know about topics that might be of interest to a professional or trade publication. Ask yourself these questions and plumb your experience and knowledge for answers:

• Do you have a relative or friend who works in a hospital that has recently begun several new approaches to improve employee relations? If yes, health care trade magazines that circulate among hospital administrators might be interested in hearing from you.

• Is your college cooperating with other institutions to develop distance learning? If yes, trade magazines reporting on new uses for technology and professional magazines aimed at educators might be interested in the program.

• Do you work part-time at a retail store that has tried new ideas for improving customer service that have paid off in increased sales? If yes, editors of trade publications designed for retail store management might be curious about the ideas.

• You fish, and you've experimented with (tested) a number of different combinations of equipment. You already have sent a piece to a consumer magazine for people like you, but did you think that a trade publication circulating among dealers in fishing equipment also might be interested in hearing from you?

• Your family bought an old house and restored it carefully and authentically. You thought a consumer magazine devoted to home decorating and furnishing might accept an article from you, but did you know several trade publications might be interested in hearing from you?

• Your full-time job is teaching first grade, and you have been trying out some new techniques for helping children with real learning problems read better, and they work! Are you aware of professional publications devoted almost exclusively to articles from teachers who have been successful with new approaches to instruction?

You get the idea. Your move.

Know Your Audience

Start out with the assumption that readers of trade and professional publications already know a great deal about their industry, business or profession. Probably as much or more than you know. Generally, they will be familiar with the terminology and jargon (or most of it) in their field. If, for example, the audience you're writing for knows something is a thingamajig and not a whatsit, you better make sure you know it, too.

• **Read the magazines for which you hope to write.** Ask editors for writers' guidelines. When you do evaluate the magazines which you are interested in, take note of the tone of writing. It probably is authoritative without being scholarly. Authors are writing to an audience that expects them to address them in their language and on the basis of personal knowledge or careful and thorough research. Authors don't write down nor up to their audience; they write to them on their level.

• **Pay attention to what editors say about their readers.** Here is how some editors describe their readers or the tone of writing in their publication, as reported by *Writer's Market 2000.*

"We are the second-oldest periodical covering space today. Our audience is the primary builders and system integrators in space, plus the top analysts and policy makers in the field." *Military Space*

"It [our publication] is written for individuals at all levels of association management, with emphasis on senior staff and CEOs." *Executive Update*

"Architecture is edited for the architects, specifiers, and design professionals responsible for designing and specifying today's new building construction, existing rehabilitation, and remodeling projects." *Architecture Magazine*

"A frequent mistake is taking too 'novice' or too 'expert' an approach. You need to know our audience well and to understand how much they know about computers." *Technology & Learning*

"Read the magazine to get a full understanding of the subject matter, the writing style [tone] and the readers. . . ." *Firehouse Magazine*

"[Writers] do not need to be computer experts, but they do have to understand how to explain the impact of the technology and the applications in which a user is involved." *Computer Graphics World*

"We require sophisticated treatment of current legal, political and social issues." *ABA Journal, The Lawyer's Magazine*

"Our core readers are managers and professionals who specialize in employee training and development. . . . We have a large secondary readership among managers of all sorts who are concerned with improving human performance in their organizations." *Training Magazine, The Human Side of Business*

FOR EXAMPLE

This article from the February 2000 issue of *Cardiology Today* illustrates the point made by John Carter of SLACK Incorporated that all SLACK news magazines include sections on practice management. Many other professional and trade magazines, perhaps most, include articles of general interest to readers that do not pertain directly to research, technical know-how or skill development in a particular profession, industry or business.

Choosing a CD-ROM program for clinical reference
by William Parmley, MD
(reprinted by permission of SLACK Inc.)
Traditionally, the way to keep up with changing medical information is by reading peer-reviewed journals. In cardiology, this requires reading 20 journals on a regular basis to stay current. The mere thought of having to read that many journals on any topic is overwhelming to say the least—an enormous undertaking that is obviously not practical. Therefore, in addition to reading journals, it is important to adopt a mechanism that is easily incorporated into your schedule and ensures that you are receiving the most current and authoritative thinking in cardiology.

Textbooks will be missing data from recent studies and scientific sessions. If your textbooks lack the most recent information and your journals are piling up, a clinical reference on CD-ROM could be an alternative.

Selecting the software
After considering the convenience of a CD-ROM clinical reference, the next step is selecting a program. First, pay careful attention to how current the information is that you will be relying on. If a program is reviewed on a daily basis, updated entirely with each release, and issued several times throughout the year, you can be assured of its timeliness.

It is also critical to investigate the data's source. Verify that the program contains an authoritative faculty and the material is peer-reviewed. Pay attention to how extensive the material is. A favorable feature that will differentiate one program from the next is the extent of recommendations.

Focus on finding a program that provides current expert commentary on a particular topic, combined with specific treatment guidelines that can be applied to your patients. The information you access should be evidence-based, but it should also go beyond that to offer guidance for a full range of questions, particularly in cases where there is little evidence.

Other features to consider are references, graphics and drug information.

Learning what to look for in a CD-ROM program is just half the battle; putting it to the test comes next.

The program should function as a virtual consultation, providing answers to patient care. Whether you need to find an alternative drug for a patient with refractory atrial fibrillation, learn the latest advances on acute therapy for myocardial infarction, review hypertrophic cardiomyopathy and get current references, or make slides and handouts on the role of beta-blockers for congestive heart failure, you should be able to rely on your CD-ROM program.

It is a constant challenge, if not an impossibility, to keep current on clinical data. I think it is essential to adopt a CD-ROM program that will allow you to easily interpret the data and apply it in a clinically meaningful way.

Robert Stowe England is a freelance writer living in Arlington, Virginia. He specializes in articles for business trade magazines, including *Banking*

Strategies, published by the Bank Administration Institute, and *Financial Executive,* published by the Financial Executives Institute. The article "Wrong-Way Exposure" is a sidebar (a short piece complementing a much longer article) that accompanied a major feature titled "Trading at Risk" that England wrote for the July/August 1999 issue of *Banking Strategies.*

"Wrong-Way Exposure"
by Robert Stowe England
(reprinted by permission of **Banking Strategies***)*
During last year's global crisis, banks discovered anew how market turmoil can undermine the credit quality of trading counter-parties, exacerbating exposure. This has prompted a new view of credit risk as more of an integral part of managing market risk. "We're trying to tie that knot even closer together," says Richard Evans, managing director and vice chairman of J.P. Morgan & Co. Inc.'s risk management committee.

J.P. Morgan uses the phrase "wrong-way exposure" to capture the way market risk can increase credit risk, which in turn can magnify the impact of market changes. Explains Evans: "The things that may cause your risk exposure to rise have a high probability of simultaneously working against the ability of the counter-party to pay." As an example, he cites a swap contract with a Thai bank possessing investment grade bonds. Any market crisis that depreciates the Thai currency, or baht, might also cause the bank's bonds to be downgraded to below-investment grade.

To safeguard against this kind of wrong-way exposure, J.P. Morgan has been stress-testing its trading counter-parties, as does BankBoston Corp. J.P. Morgan also takes a closer look at the collateral posted by trading counter-parties to cover their exposure to the bank. At one time, J.P. Morgan was satisfied with a policy that simply disallowed a trading counter-party from posting its own securities as collateral. Now, however, the bank also looks to "the relatedness question" to see if the other collateral might be prone to lose value in market events that adversely affect the counter-party. For example, J.P. Morgan might prevent a Brazilian bank from putting up the shares of another Brazilian bank as collateral since the shares of all Brazilian banks would likely decline in value in the event of a severe market shock.

When competitive pressures built up last year, some institutions allowed their trading parties to reduce or even eliminate the required "haircut" on collateral values. Prudent practice requires that the amount of collateral be adjusted as trading positions are marked to market, and that the carrying value of the collateral be discounted to better protect the bank against further unexpected drops in value. Even U.S. Treasuries are given a slight markdown of a few percentage points; more risky collateral may get a larger markdown, or haircut.

Such precautions were abandoned by banks that entered into trading contracts with the Long-Term Credit Management L.P. hedge fund. An Office of the Comptroller of the Currency analysis of last year's global crisis criticized the banks and investment banks involved with LTCM for relying too heavily "on the assumed financial strength and reputation of the principals in the firm." Compounding their error, the banks failed to obtain detailed information about the fund's trading strategy, leaving them dangerously exposed when the markets turned against LTCM.

The disarray that afflicted the world financial system last summer would have been even worse had not regulators stepped in to organize a $3.6 billion private sector rescue of LTCM. A report by the President's Working Group on Financial Markets states that if LTCM had defaulted, losses could have ranged from $300 million to $500 million for the 14 banks and securities firms who were major trading contract counter-parties or significant lenders to the fund. Even greater losses could have occurred from secondary shocks and their effect on market pricing in general.

The lesson: banks may want to avoid situations where counter-parties—such as LTCM—will not provide routine credit information. "If someone is not prepared to provide the transparency you need to enter into contracts worth tens of millions of dollars, have the courage to walk away," advises John Mastromarino, executive vice president of risk management at BankBoston.

HANDS ON

1. Browse the periodical racks of your college library and pick out four to six professional publications. Compare journals devoted primarily to research with those publications that include mostly news and feature articles about developments in the field. In the latter category note particularly articles and sections aimed at the professional who also is a business person.

   • Browse the periodical racks of your college library and pick out three or four trade publications in different fields (e.g., banking, corporate management). Note the tone of the writing. Is it authoritative without being scholarly? Do authors employ many terms and jargon peculiar to the field they are writing about? Take special note of any articles written by authors identified as freelance writers.

2. Using some of the same publications examined in Exercise 2, check the Internet to determine if these publications also have web sites. If any do, discover whether they include abstracts of articles that appear in a current or recent hard copy edition of the publication and/or complete text of articles not found in a current or recent issue.

3. Using newspaper and periodical library databases, find at least one article published within the past six months that describes some trend or important development in the world of professional and trade publications (including news of a major merger or acquisition).

3 Brainstorming Ideas

Many students of magazine article writing and beginning freelance writers in general make four basic mistakes when it comes to brainstorming ideas for articles. These are the four:

1. They overlook ideas for professional and trade publications, or ideas that might be suitable for consumer and trade/professional publications.
2. They are not sufficiently familiar with publications to know what kinds of articles editors are buying and readers are reading.
3. They rely too much on ideas based upon personal experience and are reluctant to explore ideas that may require research, especially interviews.
4. They frequently underestimate the amount of research time their idea will require if the idea is to grow into an article.

To avoid these mistakes and to improve your chances of coming up with ideas that lead to salable articles, we suggest applying a six-way test to your ideas:

- Are they fresh and timely?
- Do they have an angle?
- Are they tightly focused?
- Do they truly interest *you*?
- Are they likely to interest editors/readers of trade/professional publications as well as consumer publications?
- What research is entailed? Can you gain access to sources, and will you have time to complete all necessary research before writing the article?

This chapter explores each of these tests, and you are encouraged to reproduce, enlarge and use Table 3.1 found on page 32 to test your ideas.

TABLE 3.1 Testing Your Ideas

Testing Your Ideas

Ideas	Market	Fresh	Good Angle	You Like	Interests Readers	Tight Focus	Research Time

Determining What's New

A magazine editor flew down to North Carolina some years ago to address a freelance writers' workshop. He began his session by chastising the writers: "I read in *The New York Times* last month about a North Carolina woman who successfully landed a plane after her husband pilot died at the controls; she had never flown before. Now, ladies and gentlemen, I don't recall receiving a query from any of you suggesting an article about that event for my magazine. Why?"

The audience's response to the editor's question, if any, was not recorded. But if they did answer, they might have offered both a confession and a question of their own:

"It just never occurred to me that the event might make a magazine article."

"Considering a magazine's lead time, wouldn't an article about the event have been old hat by the time it was published?"

Old news, yes; old hat, not necessarily. The story goes to the heart of the first answer to *Idea Test Question #1: Is it fresh and timely?* Apparently, in the opinion of the magazine editor an article in his publication about the woman's heroic effort to land the plane safely would have been both fresh and timely even if it had run in the magazine months later. The reason is that the words fresh and timely are not necessarily synonymous with current or newsworthy.

The woman's accomplishment was first reported as a news event that happened yesterday: a typical newspaper account, probably an Associated Press report of three to six paragraphs. What the magazine editor presumably was looking for, and what would have made an article in his publication both fresh and timely, was an account dramatizing the event. Heroism, when described in detail and with feeling, where the central character is an ordinary person who performs extraordinary feats against almost insurmountable odds—such a story is never out of date, never old hat. Those are the ingredients of great and ever popular novels and plays.

The first thing to remember, then, is that an idea can be fresh and timely if its essential elements are timeless. Such elements, for example, as exceptional courage, boundless love (or unforgiving hatred), fearless determination, and great accomplishment.

Here are a few article ideas that meet this part of the test.

- Battling back from severe anorexia.
- Overcoming poverty and defeat to earn a high school diploma at 35.
- Working hard to make a marriage work.
- Saving a small business through perseverance and innovation.
- Playing sports five years after being told paralysis had forever made one's legs useless.

Ideas can be timely and fresh because of their timeless quality.

The second answer to Question #1 is that an idea also can be fresh and timely if it concerns a subject that is being talked and thought about. The trick here, of course, is to be reasonably sure the topic still will be hot in six to 12 months, which is when it might be published. A student once suggested a magazine article that would report local reactions to a national tragedy. That's an idea for a next-day story in the daily newspaper, but not for an article in a magazine that will be published long after the event. Another student's idea had to do with an important bill that was being argued in Congress. The problem? By the time an article appeared, the bill either could be withdrawn, still be argued, amended, defeated or enacted into law. Whatever the case, the article would not be timely.

In order to decide if something is fresh and timely, the writer must know what people are talking and thinking about. That requires the writer to first be an avid and eclectic reader, keen observer and active conversationalist. You might want to contemplate what trends and developments that were timely as we entered the 21st century may still be hot a year from now. Here are a few possibilities:

- Trigger locks. Suggested as one means of preventing purposeful or accidental killings by children who get their hands on guns. In fact, any and all proposals for reducing or eliminating random shootings in the nation may still be very timely.

- Breast cancer. Ever since national women's organizations and others focused attention on diseases affecting primarily women, almost any subject related to female health care remains a fresh topic.

- Spam. Not the virtual meat that survived WW II, but the means used by some companies to overwhelm unsuspecting e-mail users and other consumers with unsolicited and unwelcome advertising. Also a subject for state and federal investigation and, in some cases, new laws and regulations.

- Charter schools. Given national attention since the mid-nineties when President Clinton advocated them as a counter-innovation to school vouchers. Often initiated by parents and teachers, these quasi–public schools have gained acceptance in a number of states. However, some educators have argued that the movement has moved too fast, and a number of charter schools have closed because of mismanagement and other reasons.

- School vouchers. They've been on the Republican Party's wish list since the Reagan years. They have been tried in some school districts, Milwaukee, for example. They also are the object of litigation in some quarters. One issue is separation of church and state.

- Hedging. Not exactly a household word, but a high risk strategy practiced by some big money investors in the stock market that from time to time has threatened to bring down some of the nation's giant financial institutions and destabilize the national economy. Robert Stowe England, a freelance writer living in Arlington, Virginia, wrote six articles on hedging for trade publications during 1999 alone.

- Reality television. The television show about castaways was a big hit, and it spawned new shows that placed ordinary persons in situations that tested them in various ways. For example, the 2000–2001 season saw the debut of "Temptation Island" and "The Mole." Reality TV likely will continue to be expanded and hotly debated.

Remember, what's on your mind should be on other people's, too.

A Hook to Build an Idea On

An idea that might seem overdone can sometimes be made fresh and timely if you can respond positively to *Idea Test Question #2: Does it have an angle?* A new angle.

Much has been written about illicit drugs on college campuses: how bad and widespread the problem, the effect drugs are having on students' work and relationships, what college administrations are doing to control the problem, and so on. A student had a new angle: a week in the life of a drug pusher. A young man who lived next door to him was the primary supplier of drugs on campus. He gave permission to the student to shadow him daily as he arranged his buys and then made his contacts and sales. The only condition for the pusher's cooperation: "No names." The idea was fresh and, arguably, salable as an article. Unfortunately, the student's query letter to editors and his article draft did not measure up to his idea.

On the other hand, Lee Beadling had an idea with a fresh angle that led to an article, a check, and, ultimately, to a career as a successful staff writer and freelancer. When he was a student, Beadling was a new father and had care of the baby during most days when his wife worked. He soon learned that, despite today's practice whereby mothers and fathers share duties of child-rearing, many women don't really trust men with a baby. And that was the angle: Mr. Mom v. Real Moms. "It all became clear to me the day I took my two-week-old son, Kyle, to the pediatrician's office." That's how Beadling's article began in the June 1994 issue of *American Baby.* The full text of the article is included in the *For Example* section of this chapter.

Very often the right angle is achieved when the writer discovers new information or reinterprets old information about a topic, or looks at something from a new and/or different perspective. When we say new information, we mean information revealed for the first time and also information not widely known and, therefore, new to most persons—perhaps including the writer and most magazine editors.

One of the best ways to discover new information, as pointed out earlier, is by reading widely and regularly. In the fall of 1993, I came across a four-paragraph article buried on a back page of the daily newspaper. It reported that the National Park Service had been awarded a small grant to establish something called the New Jersey Coastal Heritage Trail. The trail would be a first-of-its-kind national park, stated the article, because it would consist mainly of roads connecting state parks, wildlife refuges and local historical sites. That was enough of an angle for me, and I queried *Trailer Life* magazine, whose audience is primarily owners of recreation vehicles. The article appeared in that publication the following June. I have written about the trail twice since for another magazine.

At the time of the so-called massacre at Columbine High School in Littleton, Colorado, when the nation was looking for something or someone to blame, many persons placed rock star Marilyn Manson near the top of their list of villains. It didn't help that one of the young killers was a Marilyn Manson fan. So, guess whose byline was on the article "Columbine: Whose Fault Is It?" in the June 24, 1999 issue of *Rolling Stone*? Right, Marilyn Manson. Talk about new perspectives! He wrote, "The name Marilyn Manson has never celebrated the sad fact that America puts killers on the cover of *TIME* magazine, giving them as much notoriety as our favorite movie stars." The article certainly approached that tragedy from a direction no one could have predicted. Unless of course they were the editors of *Rolling Stone.*

On a slow news day, reporters are apt to "update" or freshen an old or continuing story by calling a source or two for a few quotes that might imply new or renewed action. The resulting, "forced" article is basically a new lead paragraph followed by lots of background paragraphs. It's an old trick designed to fill a news hole that has already swallowed up all of the day's legitimate news. This technique is not suggested to magazine article writers. The angle—the hook—has to flow naturally from the idea, not be an artificial sweetener slapped on a sour idea better forgotten.

Narrowing Down

Teachers of expository writing (remember them?) tell their students to narrow down or limit a subject before writing about it. Their reasoning? "Because too broad a subject can result in a diffuse, rambling essay, be sure to restrict your general subject before starting to write." That good advice comes from the authors of *The Macmillan Writer* (Macmillan Publishing Company). The same lesson needs to be learned by magazine article writers. Be able to answer yes to *Idea Test Question #3: Is the idea tightly focused?* Photographers will tell you that panoramic shots may be great for landscapes, but closeups capture substance, action, drama.

A student wanted to write an article about the benefits of running, but there isn't much of a market, if any, for a general article about running. Then he took a closer look. What he saw in his mind's eye was the day he went out running through the woods and forgot it was opening day of the bow and arrow deer hunting season. He subsequently wrote a scary–funny article about that day: hunters in camouflage and black face jumping out from behind trees and arrows whizzing by his ears as he ran. The article was published in a national magazine.

Here are some examples of narrowing down the focus of an idea that is too broad and general:

- too broad: advantages and disadvantages of surfing the Internet
  tighter focus: many college students research the 'net incorrectly or they are addicted to surfing
- too broad: bed and breakfast inns are more popular and profitable
  tighter focus: business persons choosing B & B inns over city hotels
- too broad: what's new in hip-hop music scene
  tighter focus: successful demo gets hip-hop group out of basement
- too broad: lore of the Great Plains Indian tribes
  tighter focus: buttes over which Indians once drove buffalo herds
- too broad: recent media mergers create huge conglomerates
  tighter focus: how media conglomerates get around anti-trust laws

Finding Ideas You Like

One of the most frustrating aspects of teaching magazine article writing over the years has been to encounter so much frustration on the part of students when it comes to thinking of a topic to write about. Too often, a student will settle for an idea that he or she can't really get enthusiastic over—doesn't really care for. "I can't come up with anything I like" or "I can't think of anything else" are frequently the sad refrains. Many students, when confronted with *Idea Test Question #4, Do your ideas interest you?*, are resigned to answer, "No."

The problem is twofold, and the parts are related.

Frankly, part one of the problem has simply to do with the typical college student's life. The college student, for the most part, exists pretty much in a tight little world that is populated mostly by persons of the same age group doing primarily the same things (going to classes, studying, attending parties and campus events) and sharing many of the same interests. The college student thus absorbed and, yes, confined, hasn't much time for or much curiosity about life off campus. All that is said not as a criticism but as an observation.

The result, however, is that when students struggling to come up with an idea they like are asked, "What else are you interested in?" the response often is, "Not much." It isn't that such students are dull and shallow people; it is more the case that they do not have time or don't take time to move very far from the campus, either mentally or physically.

Part two follows. What a number of students searching for an idea they like finally settle for is a personal experience. Very often they honestly aren't really excited about the personal experience, but it's something they know and *think* will be easy to write about. Here are some examples of personal experiences that students wanted to write about even though they couldn't see much merit in the idea as a magazine article:

- How I squandered money during spring break in Florida
- How a friend and I visited eight ball parks in a week
- Why the bar where I work has been successful
- Why Michael Jordan is a hero to me and others
- Getting along with college roommates
- What I don't like about fraternity parties
- What it was like working on a farm last summer
- What the bar scene is like in (fill in name of nearby city)
- Why and how I got tattooed

Personal experience is never to be discounted or ruled out as an article idea. However, ideas based on personal experience should be put to the same tests as all other ideas. When that is done, as with the ideas listed above, they often do not measure up. You must be your first and harshest critic. If your ideas don't pass muster with you, then it makes little sense to pass them on to anyone else—especially a magazine editor.

Passing Through the Gates

Remember, editors are gatekeepers. In order for your idea to become an article in a consumer, trade or professional magazine (print or online), some editor must like it. For the editor to open the gate to the magazine, the editor must be convinced the idea, when developed into an article, will interest, entertain, and/or inspire the magazine's readers. Therefore, you must give a hopeful but honest answer to *Idea Test Question #5: Will an editor like it?*

Probably the number one reason why editors turn down article ideas submitted to them is because the articles are not appropriate for the magazine's readers. The editors further point out the reason freelance writers submit inappropriate article ideas is because they don't really know the magazine's table of contents—the kinds of topics written about in issue after issue. And writers often don't know the magazine's audience very well, if at all.

Concerning personal experience as the basis for an article idea, if you are considering a trade or professional publication, for example, you would find by studying a few magazines in the field that interests you that they are not big on personal experience. What the editors and readers of those magazines are most interested in are ideas for articles that inform—inform about new products, new processes, new developments, laws and regulations impacting the industry or profession, profiles of movers and shakers, and so on.

Here is what some editors had to say concerning article ideas:

"Many ideas we receive are too broad. What we're looking for are very specific ideas. For example, a writer suggested a general article about how to write a college essay. What I would have preferred are a few case histories about how specific students at several different institutions wrote excellent, passing essays. Student-writers have to remember they're submitting ideas to editors who have read it all, or almost all. Tell them to be creative. Tell them to submit ideas they'd like to read about in our magazine."
—Gina LaGuardia, editor-in-chief, *College Bound Magazine*

"A lot of ideas we get simply don't fit the market. The writers aren't familiar with the industry. We want nuts and bolts ideas, but many writers forget to give detailed information about their idea. My suggestion to writers submitting ideas to trade publications is to test out their premise—idea—with at least one person in the industry before sending it on to an editor."
—Tina Manzer, editorial director, *Educational Dealer, Games Retailer* and *Arts Materials Retailer*

"Read several issues of the magazine. Too often, freelance writers send in ideas that don't meet our standards. For example, we don't use articles that contain descriptive violence or sex. We have high moral standards. Also, [unlike many magazines] we want first-person articles; they account for half the magazine's contents. Stories like 'how my relatives came through Ellis Island,' and 'my father worked for Thomas Edison.' "
—Bruce Beggs, associate editor, *Grit Magazine*

"I'm a freelancer myself [for other publications], and *I* sometimes have trouble coming up with good ideas. I think it's very hard to come up with an idea on purpose. I suggest carrying around a little notebook in which the writer can jot down ideas when they occur to him or her. For example, you're watching a video that features songs by so-and-so, and you ask yourself, 'Whatever happened to so-and-so?' Well, if you have the question, songwriters who read our [trade] magazine also might be curious. Watch MTV, read *Billboard,* and so on. Above all, pay attention to what's going on. "
—Roberta Redford, publisher and editor, *Contemporary Songwriter Magazine*

"First of all, a freelance writer has to remember that we're a professional magazine, not a consumer magazine. For example, we get ideas from writers about celebrities who have undergone orthopedic surgery (e.g., Bo Jackson's hip replacement). That's not what our readers want to read about. Sometimes what works best for us is when a freelance writer calls or writes and offers to report on a conference or symposium that we can't staff. If the writer doesn't have much background in the field, it helps if the meeting is not super-technical. We also might be interested in an idea about an orthopedic surgeon who has pioneered a new technique. Freelance writers don't have to have an extensive background in medicine; in fact, we prefer writers with a journalism background. For example, people who have worked for newspapers always have a leg up."

    —Kathleen Ogle, executive editor, *Orthopedics Today*

"What works best for us are case studies about how telecommunications technology has been used to solve problems on a college campus. Also, articles about innovative ways colleges have used to raise funds to support telecommunications, or how an institution of higher education can make limited funds go farther. Technology is changing very quickly, and we're interested in articles about legislation and regulations that affect telecommunications in higher education. What I don't want are ideas about products—infomercials, really—and ideas that are too localized. We have a national audience."

    —Patricia Scott, editor, *ACUTA Journal for Telecommunications in Higher Education*

Do You Have Time for Research?

Several years ago, two students suggested different ideas for travel magazines. One wanted to write about an enchanted village off the beaten path she had visited in the mountains of southern France the year before. The other student's idea focused on a seaside community in Connecticut he had stumbled across one day and was told how it had transformed itself from an ordinary town of no special interest or attraction into an extraordinary place that was worth a special visit.

The student who wanted to write about the village in France had pleasant but not detailed or vivid memories of the town. And no notes. In short, she had forgotten many physical features—what the precious, little shops looked like; what the aromas emanating from the bakery and perfumery smelled like, what vibrant colors painted the houses hugging the streets, and how the mountains surrounding the town looked at sunrise and sunset. The other student simply had been told that the Connecticut town had undergone a kind of plastic surgery. He hadn't asked many questions or taken any notes at the time. And he had not known the community before the changeover.

Both students had the same problem. Their ideas could not be developed into articles without some rather extensive research. The student who had visited France said she would telephone a friend in or near the village and have him collect material about the village and take color slides. After receiving the materials, she would call various shop owners and others in the town for comments. Unfortunately, the time frame for completing this research was a month or more past the deadline for completing the assignment. And that was assuming (a major assumption) that all would work out as she envisioned it. The other student confessed he had no time (and, frankly, no inclination) to go back to Connecticut and spend a day or two in the reborn town on Long Island Sound. Unfortunately, then, their response had to be "No" to *Idea Test Question #6: Will you have time to complete necessary research?*

If you think of research as both collection and recollection of information, even an idea based on personal experience requires recall of events and, frequently, double-checking certain facts with other persons involved in the experience. A student wanted to write how her religious faith was tested by her terrible ordeal with the disease lupus and its complications. She thought an article about her experience might give some comfort and inspiration to others. In order to develop the idea she had to learn even more about lupus and its impact on the body than she already knew. She also had to plumb her heart and soul deeply to come up with tough questions prompted by real fear and honest answers based on her faith. It took more time than she had imagined.

Many students are surprised when they discover how long it takes just to arrange for necessary interviews. Typical comments: "The person I need to talk to can't see me until the week after next," "I keep playing phone tag with the person who has the information I need," "I thought I needed to talk to one person, but now I find out there are a couple of others I have to see."

Research is covered in a later chapter, but for now take note: When testing your article ideas, be as honest and foreseeing as you possibly can be in estimating the time you will need for research. Then add some days to your first, best estimate.

FOR EXAMPLE

Here are three examples of students' article ideas that passed the six tests and were received favorably by a magazine editor.

• A student's parents had been raised in Germany during World War II and were brainwashed into believing Nazi propaganda about Jews. Tragically, they were never cleansed of the lies, and they passed them on to their daughter—the student. The summer previous to her enrolling in the magazine article writing course, the student had worked as a camp counselor and accompanied a group of children on a field trip to Washington, D.C. Their last stop was the Holocaust Museum. The museum exhibits impact powerfully on every visitor, but the student emerged totally devastated. She realized for the first time that her parents had lied to her while she was growing up—teaching her to hate and despise Jews ("they got what they deserved"). Her world was turned upside down.

The student queried *INSIDE, the Jewish Exponent Magazine.* The editor asked her to write the article. Later, the editor returned the article with suggestions for rewrite before publishing. Unfortunately, the student did not follow through.

• A student's grandmother kept all the greeting cards sent to her by her husband (the student's grandfather) during the 1930s and 1940s when they were first going together and later when they were married. The student contrasted sentiments expressed 50 and 60 years ago with those contained in cards today to show how relationships between men and women have changed over the years. An editor at Hallmark cards aided the student's research.

GRIT: American Life and Traditions liked the idea and asked to see the article. However, the magazine's editor decided the article required too much revision to meet the magazine's format. The student, who has since graduated, plans to resubmit the idea to other publications, possibly some women's magazines.

• Lee Beadling's article, "The Man With the Baby," was written as an assignment for the Magazine Article Writing course at Glassboro State College (now Rowan University) in the summer of 1993 and published in the June 1994 edition of *American Baby* magazine. The angle, or hook, for this personal experience story is implied in the title. Here is a father's story in a magazine where the articles mostly are about mothers and their babies. While the feature is about the experiences of a father, the anecdotes cited primarily tell of the father's encounters with mothers. The editors must have agreed with Beadling that the article zinged a few pointed messages mothers (the magazine's primary readers) needed to hear.

"The Man With the Baby"
by Lee Beadling
(reprinted by permission of the author)
It all began to become clear to me the day I took my two-week-old son, Kyle, to the pediatrician's office. Heads turned as we entered the packed waiting room. Struggling with an overloaded diaper bag in one hand and my sleeping baby in the other, I found an empty seat and sat down, bumping Kyle's head on the armrest in my descent. Kyle woke and began to wail. Across the room a heavy-set woman with a ruddy complexion peeled a toddler from her lap and came over to me.

"Looks like somebody's hungry," she said, looming over us as the rest of the waiting room occupants looked on.

"Um, no, he just bumped his head," I said, ashamed. "Just a little, on the armrest." I glanced down at the offending armrest as if trying to assign blame.

"Maybe he's wet," suggested the mother beside me. "Did you think to change him?" I smiled an uneasy smile.

The heavyset woman took Kyle from me. "There, now, don't cry," she crooned. "Your daddy just didn't know what he was doing, that's all."

Didn't know what I was doing? Didn't think to change him? Who did these women think I was? This was my son!

As the nontraditional family becomes more traditional, men with babies are becoming a more frequent sight. However, since most people still look upon mothers as the parent who *really* knows how to care for children, the problems of being a man with a baby are seldom addressed. Those of us guys holding diaper bags face some pretty stiff criticism, and some damaging assumptions, as my experience showed me.

Becoming Mr. Mom

My wife returned to work shortly after Kyle was born. Since I work a swing shift and she works nine to five, we agreed that I would care for Kyle while she was at the office. I had no experience with child care. I would learn on the job.

One of my first lessons was to accept the fact that all babies cry. Most men, myself included, like to be in control of their emotions and surroundings at all times, and a crying baby tends to quickly erode feelings of mastery. It took some time, but after a while I figured out the meanings of most of Kyle's wails.

But when Kyle would cry in public, women around me seemed to assume that I needed their assistance. I had to swallow my pride as I was instructed on how to care for my son.

Men, I like to think, have come to accept women as doctors, lawyers and judges, yet many women, at least in my experience, find it difficult to accept a man with a baby, and no mommy in sight.

One day shortly after my wife returned to work, a friend and I went out to lunch. Soon after we ordered, Kyle decided to voice his displeasure with this new, unfamiliar environment. My friend, unaccustomed to young children, tried to ignore Kyle's cries, but it quickly became apparent that the attention we were calling to ourselves was causing him some embarrassment.

Our waitress came to the table and asked if everything was all right. Obviously, she saw two men and a baby and assumed they must need help, so she offered to hold Kyle. I didn't want to give in—after all, I could soothe my own child! But then I looked at my friend, who was silently pleading with me to give the baby to the waitress. I reluctantly handed him over, and they disappeared behind the kitchen doors.

Obviously relieved, my friend launched into a one-sided conversation that I completely ignored. How could I have done that? Where was my son? As time wore on, my mild panic gave way to complete terror. My mind filled with every fear a parent could have. What if the waitress was a deranged person? What if she was back there right now, putting Kyle in a soup pot? What if. . . .

But before our salads were even served, the kitchen doors swung open and the waitress reappeared with my son, now cooing lightly and chewing on a plastic spoon.

"I think he's cutting a tooth. You should have your wife get something for that," the waitress said.

Get something for that? My fear rapidly turned to anger. Why should she have assumed I don't know how to handle a teething baby?

Woes of a Dad on the Go

Aside from these incidents, I've faced another, more practical problem in being an at-home dad—finding adequate changing facilities.

One day Kyle needed a diaper change in the library. I took him to the men's room, only to discover that the sink was about as clean as what you'd find on a prison ship. I ended up performing a balancing act, sitting on the toilet bowl, Kyle lying in my lap, his head dangling. That day I learned the secret: be prepared. From then on I never left the house without an extra crib sheet or beach towel to provide a clean changing surface.

Another niggling note: most diaper bags are designed with babies and women in mind. Those that aren't covered with ducks and bunnies look like women's pocketbooks. I alternate between a "studly"-looking gym bag and a studious backpack.

Now Kyle is 15 months old and toddling around by himself, and I've discovered that the man with the toddler is not nearly as conspicuous as the man with the infant, but I still get an occasional tip from the moms I meet. But now I can dish it right back.

H A N D S   O N

1. Roberta Redford, editor of *Contemporary Songwriter Magazine* and also a freelance writer for other publications, said she carries a small notebook with her at all times to jot down article ideas when they occur to her. Use your own notebook and, over a period of weeks, record any article ideas that pop into your head as you go about your daily routine. These ideas might be suggested by news stories, conversations with friends or relatives, movies and TV shows watched, personal experience, special skills or knowledge you or someone you know possesses, and so on.

   • Next, go through the ideas and weed out those ho-hum personal experience ideas that reflect ordinary events in the life of a college student.

   • Consider which of the ideas might be developed for a trade or professional publication. Which ones could be written for both a consumer and a trade publication?

   • Apply the six-way test to each idea. Be tough!

   • Match each idea that passes the test with one or more appropriate magazines. Don't forget e-zines/web zines.

2. Leaf through two consumer magazines and one trade or professional magazine; also scroll down an e-zine/web zine. Select one or two articles in each publication. As best you can, answer these questions about them:

   • What is the angle?

   • Why is it fresh and timely?

   • How did the author narrow the focus?

CHAPTER

4 Researching Thoroughly

If you sat down with a group of magazine editors—consumer, trade, or professional—and you asked them what one word of advice they would give to students of magazine article writing concerning research, their unanimous answer would be "more." If they put their answer in writing, the word would be in caps, underlined, and followed by exclamation points galore.

Perhaps a writer can research too much, but the common problem, constantly complained of by editors, is that most writers, particularly those new to the profession, conduct far too little research. And not infrequently they seek out the wrong sources and ask the wrong questions—or not enough of them.

Chapter three pointed out that one of the tests to determine if your ideas are right for a magazine is whether you will have enough time to research thoroughly. So many students of magazine article writing come up with ideas that would, if developed properly, take far too long to research.

What Editors Say

A group of editors was asked to name the primary fault they find with writers' research. Here are their responses:

- "Not detailed enough. You have to know everything before you can choose the angle, find the sterling quote, and the nugget that makes the story worth printing."
  —Donna Doyle, editor-in-chief, *Grit Magazine*

- "Sloppy, not complete."
  —Roberta Redford, publisher/editor, *Contemporary Songwriter*

- "Too many indications of not having seen or read the publication to which they are trying to sell an article."
  —Jon C. Halter, editor, *Scouting Magazine*

- "Fail to ask for enough explanations from sources, so that when I query a point, they say, 'I wondered that, too.' "
  —Whitney Wood, managing editor, *NurseWeek* and *HealthWeek*

- "Lack of fact checking, spell checking, and providing enough sources."
  —Julia Bencomo Lobaco, editor, *Vista Magazine*

- "It [thorough research] doesn't exist, or only a few sources are used, and those few are used solely to support the author's bias. Author [sometimes] only 'rounds up the usual suspects' in presenting sides of an issue, keeping [the article] superficial."
  —Tom Bowden, managing editor, *Tech Directions*

- "Too cursory. Now, with the Internet, researchers have become extremely lazy in their efforts!"
  —Lesley S. Abravanel, managing editor, *Porthole Cruise Magazine*

- "Not digested and incorporated neatly into the article."
  —David Heim, executive editor, *The Christian Century*

- "Surprisingly, many [writers] aren't fully utilizing the method of phone interviews. They're solely relying on e-mail correspondence, press releases, book excerpts, etc. From there, they're drawing their own conclusions, forgetting the elements of basic attribution."
  —Gina LaGuardia, editor-in-chief, *College Bound Magazine*

- "Not *enough*! They need to track down lots of sources, not just one or two. [They] need to not take the easy way out."
  —Tina Manzer, editorial director, *Educational Dealer* and *Games Retailer*

- "Without adequate time to learn and research an article, their [the writers'] 'interpretation' of facts or events—even quotes—causes the article to be inaccurate."
  —Tom Hamilton, editor, *Balloon Life*

How Research Begins

Research almost always begins with the writer asking two key questions:

1. **"What information do I need to find out, or learn?"**
2. **"Where do I find the information?"**

These two questions help organize a series of research tips and strategies based on the comments by the editors surveyed, the advice of other editors, and the experience of professional writers and students.

1. "What information do I need to find out, or learn?"

Tip one: be curious. Teachers are both amazed and dismayed how the insatiable curiosity that drives young children to ask a dozen "why" questions per hour (sometimes driving their parents and teachers to distraction) seems almost to have disappeared by the time those children reach their teens and twenties. Bruce Ballenger, in his book *The Curious Researcher* (Allyn & Bacon, 1994), speaks to college students about the typical research paper they will write, but he could be addressing students of magazine article writing as well: "Whatever condition it's in, your curiosity must be the driving force behind your research. . . . It's the most essential ingredient."

Tip two: don't forget anything.

The tendency when answering the first question is to think of one or two pieces of information needed and let it go at that. Before plunging into the Internet, consulting a database or arranging the first interview, take enough time to answer the question as fully as possible. Jot down anything and everything you conceivably might need. It could be—probably should be in most cases—a long list. It might include comparative statistics, historical background and dates, biographical data, case studies and other kinds of illustrations and examples, authoritative opinions and rulings, applicable laws and regulations, governing policies, definitions or explanations of technical terms and procedures, how something or somebody works, and what others have observed or experienced.

Very often, the information needed includes whatever it takes to provide a broad or larger perspective for the article in question. Consider these examples:

• A professional writer working on an article about the first Jewish agricultural settlement in America needed a considerable number of historical documents in the form of memoirs, correspondence, newspaper clippings, and so on to learn, generally, why and how the settlement came about and its place in the immigration movements of the time.

• A student was seriously injured in an amusement park accident, sued the park owner and ride operator, and lost in court. Her article idea focused on what she learned from the experience that others might profit from (e.g., taking down names and addresses of witnesses). In order to place her personal experience in perspective, she at least needed national statistics on the number of amusement park accidents and injuries for the previous year or for some other period.

• A New Jersey casino, bothered by underage boys and girls trying to sneak onto the gambling floor, devised a dramatic program for advising students not yet 18 in the state's high schools that they were not permitted on the casino floor and could face serious consequences if caught. The student who wanted to write about the program also needed to find out what the experience and policy of the U.S. casino industry in general is regarding underage "gamblers."

• A student suffers from panic attacks. Once she became hysterical on a ferry that had just left port. She demanded the captain return to the dock. (He did.) The student wanted to write about panic disorder. Of course, she knew about her own condition and experiences, but she needed to know a lot more about panic disorder: how extensive it is nationwide, its manifestations, what the latest treatments are, and so on.

2. Where do I find the information?
Strategy one: surf the Internet—but cautiously and wisely

A student in a course on research and argument drafted this thesis: "Students now conduct most or all their research on the Internet; because much of what is contained on the Internet may not be credible, students' papers may also become less credible in the future." The student put his finger on one of the problems inherent in Internet research. The other problem is number of hits—a zillion information sites that may be listed in response to one or two keywords.

Here are two important points to remember about information on the Internet:

1. Almost anyone can publish almost anything on an Internet web site.
2. Whereas paper text (contained in books and other printed materials) is almost always subject to fact-checking and editing by someone other than the author, cybertext may not be scrutinized and questioned by a second party.

Given this situation, here are some helpful suggestions for evaluating cybertext:

Check out the author and his/her affiliation. In the case of books, periodicals and newspapers, an author usually is known to one or more editors who not only can vouch for the author's credibility but may have selected the author because of his/her credentials. The editors usually are also aware of the author's affiliations and any biases that may result from such affiliations. For example, if a writer offers a magazine an article on social or political issues of the day, the editor would surely know, or find out, what bias or slant to expect if the author listed his/her affiliation with or reliance on the source People for the American Way. The name sounds as if it might possibly be a conservative organization.

One way to check out an organization is to click on its web site. The home page of People for the American Way first states that the organization works "to promote full citizen participation in our democracy and safeguard the principles of our country from those who threaten the American dream." That message still smacks of conservatism. Later on, however, the home page refers to the organization's monitoring of the religious right and conservative media. Finally, we see the organization's true colors: red, white, and liberal blue.

You can find out information about an author and his/her affiliation from a number of sources. Here are some of them:

American National Biography (print)
Directory of American Biography (print)
Who's Who (print)
Biographical Index (online)
Encyclopedia of Associations (print)
Associations—Nonprofit (online)

A good source of information about organizations that do business in the nation's capital—and nearly all of them do at some time or other—is the *Washington Information Directory* published by Congressional Quarterly, Inc.

Check the date of information. Many students and other researchers have assumed that nearly everything that appears on the Internet is current. Wrong! Sometimes no date is listed. If you encounter information with no date, do the following: (1) Read the information carefully for any clues as to date (e.g., reference to events) and (2) Compare to one or more other sources that provide similar information to see if they give a date.

Determine the accuracy and reliability of the information.

This task is made easier, of course, if you have been able to learn what you need to know about the author and his/her affiliation. Referring to People for the American Way again, once you have determined from its web site that the organization is national, has been around for almost 20 years, publishes newsletters, and has testified before Congress and elsewhere, you may assume that its information is probably accurate and reliable—albeit with a liberal slant.

Successful research on the Internet (and also on databases), particularly if you are not going to specific web sites, depends on your punching in appropriate keywords in the search box. Unfortunately, the Internet (and databases) don't always use the same terms that you might use. For example, a few years ago I was asked to collect general information about senior citizens for a friend who was considering publishing a newsletter aimed at that population. I went to the Internet and various databases. In each case I typed in the keywords senior citizens and came up empty—zero hits. I couldn't believe it! The term senior citizen has become as common to the language as teenager or adolescent. I finally struck the mother lode of information when I typed in the words aging and aged. I think the rationale for using these terms that most researchers would not think of first (maybe not even second or third) might be that most state governments and the federal government have offices on aging.

Here are two tips on selecting the right keywords:

Be as precise as possible. This can help you avoid either coming up with no hits or too many. One way to accomplish this is to rely on Library of

Congress headings. These are found in large, red books (ask the reference librarian). If you look up a word in the books (volumes are organized alphabetically), you will find broader, narrower, and related terms for the word you selected. This can help you be more precise in your search.

Be prepared with half a dozen or more keyword combinations. For example, suppose you were looking for information on teenage culture. That particular combination of words probably will get you nothing; the Internet and databases don't recognize the existence or reality of something called teenage culture. But you might find some of what you're looking for by typing in such combinations as teenagers/music, teenagers/lifestyle, and teenagers/consumerism and by substituting the word adolescents for teenagers in the combinations.

Strategy two: interview knowledgeable persons

Typically, in most college courses that require research, students limit their inquiries to print and cyber-sources. On the other hand, students writing for magazines and newspapers often look to people sources: persons who not only can contribute their knowledge and experience, but whose impromptu responses to questions from the writer serve to enliven and energize the prose. Bruce Ballenger, in his book *The Curious Researcher,* reminds student researchers/writers not to "underestimate the value of 'live' and other non-library sources. Authorities don't just live in books."

Even the casual reader of magazines soon discovers that the authors of many articles have relied heavily on interviews with persons whose expertise is primarily responsible for whatever authority or credibility the article has. Frequently, the experiences and observations of interviewees give an article its "personality": what it's really like to create a unique national park from scratch; to advise leaders of brand new democracies how to write a constitution for the first time; to reform a beat-up, beaten-down urban high school.

Here are a few examples of why and how student and professional writers have relied on people sources:

• A student wanted to write an article about a popular outdoor pageant presented annually by residents in a southern region of the United States. She had witnessed the pageant and collected brochures about it, but one thing in particular was missing. She needed to find out what it is like for an ordinary citizen of the region—e.g., a teacher, auto mechanic, homemaker—to play a man or woman who helped shape the history and culture of the region over the centuries.

• The same professional writer working on the article about the Jewish settlement wanted to know what it was like to live in the settlement during its early years. Since the original adult settlers were deceased, he needed to talk to their children. Perhaps they could tell him what it was really like growing up in the settlement—playing in a nearby river while their mothers washed the family's clothes, surviving harsh winters when firewood was in short supply, and so on.

- A professional writer was working on an article about a program in Baltimore designed for young mothers living in low-income projects who had dropped out of high school and now desired to earn a diploma. The city school administration provided materials describing the program, including data evaluating its results. What the writer needed was personal accounts of women who had benefited from the program.

- A student who worked part-time in a bank wanted to write a magazine article about how senior citizens have been bedazzled by today's computerized banking services. She knew how the technology worked, but she needed to talk to customers of a certain age who still feel uncomfortable banking by phone.

Steps to a Profitable Interview

An unplanned interview is rarely, if ever, successful. The interviewer needs to follow a series of steps to ensure that the interviewee provides whatever background information, anecdotes, descriptions, feelings, and so on that may be stored in the brain or remembered by the heart.

Step one: choose the interviewee carefully. Always refer back to the first research question: What information do I need to find out, or learn? Selecting the right person(s) to interview depends largely on your answer to that question. For example, the student writing about the pageant needed to know what it's like for a person with no professional acting experience to play a role in such a major production. She couldn't get "live" answers to that "lively" question from either print or cyber-sources.

Of course, you want to select someone who not only has something to say but also is willing and able to say it. You hope these qualities can be determined when the potential interviewee is first contacted, but sometimes you are fooled. In such cases, it may not be until the interview is well underway that you discover (1) the interviewee doesn't know as much or hasn't experienced as much as you were led to believe, (2) the person can't articulate very well, and/or (3) the interviewee unexpectedly refuses to reveal what it is you came to get.

The best advice is to sound out the potential interviewee at the initial contact—when you arrange for the interview at a later time and date. Explain clearly and fully what information, etc. you are looking for and why you think this person can supply it. Sometimes you find out quickly that you have the wrong source. This may be true especially if you need to interview someone in a large organization (e.g., government or business department) and you aren't sure who on staff has the information you want. In such cases, it is helpful to first speak to someone in the public information (or public/press relations) office. Persons in that department usually are used to dealing with reporters and editors who don't have time to be routed from one phone and cubicle to another. Therefore, they often can direct a caller to the most appropriate staff member.

Step two: arrange for the interview in advance. In-person interviews are best. Telephone interviews are second best, and e-mail interviews are not recommended for reasons explained later. Regardless of the interview mode, however, your meeting with the interviewee should be carefully arranged in advance—and reconfirmed later. You want the interviewee to set aside a block of time for you, which usually won't amount to much more than 15 or 20 minutes. You have a window of opportunity that the interviewee is willing to open, but which may be closed promptly and arbitrarily when the interviewee perceives your time is up.

If the interview will be face-to-face, you need to set a location, date, and time for the interview. If the interview will take place in the interviewee's workplace or home, be sure to get specific directions, including suite, office, or apartment numbers. Sometimes it is even important to find out what elevator to take and which way to turn after getting off the elevator. I have been in federal buildings in Washington and office buildings in large cities where corridors seem to be endless and banks of elevators are at either ends of the corridors and in the middle. Knowing which elevator to take and which way to turn when exiting becomes important. Taking the wrong elevator and making the wrong turn can cost precious minutes, and busy interviewees don't have a lot of minutes to spare.

Deciding the date and time is essential for any interview. The interviewee, for example, may have only two days during the next two weeks when he or she will not be in meetings or out of town, or the person may say that Mondays and Fridays are bad, or that that it is almost impossible to set aside any time after the work day gets underway at 9 o'clock in the morning and before 4 o'clock in the afternoon. I have been advised by a number of interviewees that I must interview by telephone to call at 7:30 or 8 in the morning or between 4:30 and 5 in the afternoon. Occasionally, lunch hour is a good time to interview in-person or by telephone. What is important is to be as precise as possible about day and time.

Again, whether the interview will be conducted in-person or by telephone, the arrangements should be made in advance and reconfirmed either by mail, telephone, fax, or e-mail. Let me tell you my sad story about the time I did not take my own advice. I had arranged for an interview more than a month in advance with a former *New York Times* editor who had an office on Madison Avenue in Manhattan. I set the day and time with him personally, but I never reconfirmed the appointment. On the day set aside for the interview, I drove from my home into the city (three hours) and arrived at his office slightly before the appointed hour (a good idea). When I announced myself to the receptionist, she looked puzzled and asked why I didn't know that my interviewee had suffered a stroke and would be out of commission for another month or two. Of course, if I had reconfirmed the date and time at least the day before the appointment, I would have learned what had happened and would not have wasted a day (and a hefty parking bill).

Another very good reason for reconfirming an appointment is to provide you with the evidence if you arrive on the agreed-upon day and time only to be told that your interviewee forgot the appointment, didn't write it down, or "something came up." Your copy of the letter or e-mail reconfirming the appointment may be what you need to get back on the interviewee's schedule. A story with a happier ending occurred some years ago when I arranged for an interview in Washington and arrived on time to discover that the interviewee had been handed a last-minute assignment by her boss and now claimed she no longer had time to see me. I produced my confirmation letter and said I had come a long way to meet with her. While the resulting interview was somewhat disjointed because she had to juggle her boss's assignment, at least it took place and I got what I came for.

Step three: carefully prepare for the interview. Again, remember that first research question: What information do I need to find out, or learn? The answer to that question will determine what questions you will ask the interviewee. Some writers compose specific questions in advance of the interview. Others write down only areas for questioning. Inexperienced interviewers/writers do well to put down specific questions before conducting the interview.

Let's assume you are the student who wanted to interview by telephone a first-grade teacher who, for a month or so in the summer, becomes a character in the southern pageant depicting regional history. The student wanted to learn, of course, what it is like to take on such a role. The student decided to write down specific questions—questions like these:

- Have you had acting experience?
- How do you find time for rehearsals and performances?
- Is your family supportive and how do they adjust to your schedule?
- What character(s) do you play?
- How do you prepare yourself for the part?
- What is your costume and makeup?
- If you tell your students what you are doing, how do they react?
- Since this is an outdoor pageant, what provisions are made, if any, for excessive heat or thunderstorms?
- How do audiences react to the pageant and your performance, and how does audience reaction vary from day to day or week to week?
- What unusual experiences have you had as an actor in the pageant?

Step four: control your interview. You've selected the right person to interview, arranged for the interview in advance, and drafted questions you expect to ask. You show up (or call on the telephone) at the appointed hour. You are now at the toughest part of the process. It's easy to lose control of the interview almost from the beginning and walk away (or hang up) at the end with the distinct—and probably correct—impression that you didn't get what you were looking for. Here are a series of tips designed to make your interviews productive:

For an in-person interview, bring a note pad, a couple of pens or pencils, and a tape cassette recorder. Small, inexpensive recorders that pick up speakers very clearly, even at some distance, are available at a number of retail outlets. Also, bring an extra battery and cassette. The value of the recorder is to back up your notes and to allow you to quote the interviewee accurately. If you are conducting a telephone interview, you may still be able to use a recorder with an attachment to the receiver. *If you do this, make sure you advise the interviewee that you are recording the interview.* When we say that the recorder can back up your notes, you must remember that the interview places great demands upon you. With each question you ask, you are required to do three things all at the same time: (1) listen carefully to the answer, (2) take notes on the answer, and (3) be ready to ask the next question (which may be a follow-up question not on the list you prepared in advance).

Concerning follow-up questions and interview control, while it is necessary to have questions prepared in advance, you must remain flexible; be prepared to go in other directions. It is not only possible, but probable, that the person you're interviewing will respond to one of your questions with an answer that leads the interview in a direction you didn't anticipate, but which seems promising. I once interviewed a law professor who also served as a consultant to a number of nations trying to become democracies. He advised them on how to compose a constitution to guide them on their new course. During the interview, he casually mentioned that he collected soap from each hotel he stayed in around the world. I pursued this aside and discovered he had recently sold his soap collection to Ripley's "Believe It or Not!" Museum. I wrote about this very interesting person for two magazines, and one wanted to feature the soap collection in the lead.

Remember, the interview belongs to you. You are there for a purpose, to collect specific information for an article you intend writing. Don't allow the interviewee to wrest control of the interview from you. Normally, the interviewee does not purposely steer you off course, although this can happen if your questions probe a subject the interviewee doesn't want to discuss. Usually, it simply is a case where the interviewee has his or her own agenda. You want to talk about X; he or she wants to expound on Y. Before you can say "I'm losing control of this interview," you have. In such instances, you must politely, but firmly, get the conversation back on your track. Your line at this point might begin, "That's very interesting, but. . . ."

Be persistent without being rude. One of the problems with a telephone interview, in particular, is that it is easier for the interviewee to break it off than if the interview was in-person. The interviewee can cut short the interview with such lines as "I have a call waiting" or "someone's waiting to see me," and there's no way for you to know if there is in fact someone waiting. On the other hand, when the interviewee is facing you, those lines don't work as well. In any event, make every effort to continue a productive interview at least to the end of the time period agreed upon. Don't let the interviewee off the hook if you can help it. Stick to your questioning.

At some point during the interview, the interviewee might say, "This is off the record," meaning he or she does not wish to be quoted. The "some point" is critical. If, for example, a person agrees to be interviewed and then announces at the start of the interview that he or she does not want to be quoted directly on anything he or she will say during the interview, you have two options:

1. Respond that you do not want to conduct the interview on that basis.
2. Decide that you can use the information as background for your article without referring to the person as the source.

Suppose the interviewee announces at the end of the interview, "Oh, by the way, everything I said has to be off the record; don't quote me." Again, you have options.

1. Respond that you were not informed in advance that the interview would be off the record. If you had been, you would not have conducted the interview. At this point, you have no recourse other than to quote the person according to your notes.

2. A variation on option one is to go over the interview and your notes with the interviewee and mutually decide what can or cannot be quoted. The interviewee, upon reflection, may only have a problem with one or two statements made during the interview.

3. Again, abide by the interviewee's wishes and use the information as best you can without attribution.

If, during the interview, the interviewee asks not to be quoted in response to a particular question, make your decision on the spot: (1) Politely ask the person not to respond if the answer cannot be quoted, or (2) Agree to use the response only as background information without attribution.

It is important to note that in the case of all options, you are the one making the final decision. You are still in control.

The main problem with interviewing by e-mail is the difficulty the interviewer has controlling the interview and obtaining the information desired and as quickly as possible. Suppose, for example, you arrange to interview the first grade teacher who plays a role every summer in the southern historical pageant. You send her questions via e-mail. One of the questions asks her to name the character she plays. This is what happens next:

- In her first e-mail response, she forgets to answer that key question.
- You again e-mail the question.
- She responds, "I play an older woman."
- You respond, "Can you be more specific?"
- She responds, "A woman who spent her life in the mountains. She never went to school but raised 10 children."
- You respond, "How does the character fit into the pageant? Does she appear with her children? What about her husband? Has she raised the children alone? Is the character supposed to represent an aspect of southern life the author(s) of the pageant wish to emphasize in some way?"

You get the idea. This kind of back and forth could go on for a long time and still not be very productive. It would be far easier to get your answers to these questions via a telephone interview. An in-person interview, of course, would be best, if that were possible in this instance.

Strategy three: pay attention to detail

One way to think about this strategy is to imagine two heads facing each other drawn on a blackboard. One head represents a writer and the other a reader. It is the goal of the writer to impart what she knows, feels and believes into the head of the reader accurately and completely (draw arrow from writer's head to reader's). The only tools the writer has to accomplish this rather monumental task are words. If the writer doesn't have enough words or has not carefully chosen them, the communication breaks down. The reader doesn't believe for lack of evidence, doesn't quite understand for lack of full explanation, doesn't see for lack of precise description, doesn't react for lack of words that would evoke the appropriate emotion.

"Writing well is never easy," wrote Robin A. Cormier in her book *Error-Free Writing* (Prentice Hall, 1995). "Most people—even professional writers—would agree that writing is a skill that does not come naturally. It requires great effort to combine creativity and attention to detail in a way that results in a product that people can read and understand without effort."

Here are a series of tips that may help you pay necessary attention to detail as you research your article ideas:

Collect enough compelling evidence that your readers will have reason to believe you.

A student wrote an article whose lead promised that the article would show readers—presumably all members of just-out-of-the-basement rock bands—how they could double their fans and latch on to good marketing ideas. The writer offered three suggestions: play gigs where teenagers hang, enter Internet chat rooms where teenagers are likely to hang, and hang with other and better rock bands. The writer closed by reminding his readers to thank him for the great ideas when their fans doubled in number. What was lacking, of course, was any solid—even semi-solid—evidence that any of those ideas actually paid off.

Another student wanted to explain how today's hospitals must compete in the marketplace by demonstrating they are "family friendly." Unfortunately, the student's research was too limited; she talked briefly on the telephone to the person in charge of public relations (PR) at one hospital. The story idea had merit, but it required a number of examples of successful PR and marketing strategies to convince readers that being "family friendly" was indeed the key to survival in the health care industry.

On the other hand, Marie Faust Evitt, writing in the May 1999 issue of *Parents* magazine, interviewed or read the research findings of four different child psychologists and developmental specialists before writing her article offering readers three "tested" ways for dealing with children's misbehavior aside from spanking. She also interviewed three mothers who had tried the methods.

On page 36 of the August 2, 1999 issue of *The New Yorker*, writer/historian Michael Ignatieff ended his article on the NATO war against the Serbs by stating: "The political leaders of NATO spoke the language of ultimate commitment and practiced the warfare of minimum risk." He could rightly expect his readers to accept this conclusion because the article showed he had spent considerable time shadowing and interviewing General Wesley Clark, NATO commander, and poring over a vast array of correspondence, reports, and other materials pertaining to NATO's conduct of the war.

"Writers must know things," stated Richard Mairus in his book *A Writer's Companion* (McGraw-Hill, 1999). What he went on to warn writers about was making generalizations, drawing conclusions, and arguing a point without sufficient evidence to support their claims.

Connect Point A to Point B.

Sometimes communication breaks down because the writer has not provided the information necessary to allow readers to easily and knowingly bridge the gap between ideas, incidents, events, and so on.

A student wrote about a trip to Florida during spring break when he and his friends stopped at a service station for gasoline and then went next door to where a man was running a dart game that promised a big payoff if players hit the right spots on the board. In two paragraphs, the student described playing the game. In the next paragraph he and his friends returned to the car, their wallets considerably lighter, and convinced they had been conned. The missing link was an explanation of what about the game, the man's behavior, or their losses made them conclude they had been taken.

In his fine article on the history of disco in the November 1999 issue of *American Heritage,* Peter Braunstein begins by describing the discotheque as a "den of resistance in Nazi-occupied France." The majority of the article is devoted to disco in the United States, but instead of simply saying disco moved, or migrated, to America from France in a particular year, Braunstein provides a little anecdote to connect New York to Paris: "The man most responsible for bringing [disco] to America was Olivier Coquelin, a French expatriate whose heroism during the Korean War had earned him American citizenship. Coquelin sized up the languishing New York nightclub scene and decided that the era's wealthy jet-set clubgoers needed an alternative to the staid environment of the Stork Club and El Morocco. Thus was conceived Le Club, the first American discotheque, which opened on New Year's Eve, 1960."

Observe everything and record everything.

Remember, your readers must see, smell, feel, and hear every sight, odor, sensation and noise you experience. But they won't unless you give them the right words based on your research notes.

A student wrote about training for professional wrestlers: "Before you can work the crowds and grope loose women while generating cheers from adoring audiences, you have to get tough, get in shape and even (gulp) go to school. Wondering where on earth you're going to find a school like that? Look no farther than Mantua, New Jersey—the location of the nationally acclaimed Monster Factory."

It was obvious from the article the student had visited the Monster Factory, but nowhere did the student's readers ever see what the Monster Factory looked like, how it must have smelled of sweat and rubbing alcohol, or how it sounded when one monster threw another to the floor.

Another student wrote about his visit to an antique shop and gave us a sense of the place and a portrait of its proprietor: "The place smelled like my grandmother's house—old and musty. Beyond a huge cash register that probably dated to the 1800s I found an old man peeking over the counter at me. His NASCAR baseball cap sent shadows over his face, allowing me to see only his [full] gray mustache and cold, blue eyes. He was wearing a pair of overalls, and his untied work boots rested on the only empty spot on the counter."

Scott Raab wrote in the February 1997 issue of *GQ* about former Chicago Bulls player Dennis Rodman's visit to a Miami show bar after a basketball game: "The show is about to begin. The rows of folding chairs in front of the small stage at the back of the room remain utterly empty. Rodman hangs barside, hunched on a stool, downing kamikazes. After each round is poured—I count six in an hour—he clinks glasses with one and all and gulps his down clean. A Divine look-alike, mammoth in a black sheath, opens the revue, lip-synching and stomping in place to some campy show tune while her bosom struggles vainly to pour over the thin fabric. Mimi's next, vamping, hands on hips, but too fettered by her corset to strut her ersatz stuff. Rodman sits gaping at the stage, heavy lidded, expressionless."

Based on your interview notes (and tape cassette), develop verbatim running dialogue where and when appropriate.

A student wrote a very funny article about how his and his fiancee's life changed abruptly when they discovered after a hospital examination that she was eight months pregnant. She had shown no symptoms until then. Their wedding was two months away. One of the first things he did was to call his mother with the news. He set up the telephone conversation as follows:

"Hi mom, I'm calling from the hospital."

"Oh my God! I knew if you continued driving so fast you'd . . . "

"No mom, I'm okay. It's about Jane."

"Oh my God, what's happened?"

"Well, she's all right. It's just that . . . that she . . . we're expecting a baby."

"Oh? That's nice. When's Jane due?"

"Just before the wedding."

"Oh my God!"

Of course, the student in this instance knew the dialogue from his own experience, but the same technique can work for a writer in almost any situation where the running dialogue helps readers feel the emotion of the moment. It is, frankly, a style device used by fiction writers, but it is worth borrowing occasionally for a non-fiction article.

A variation on this kind of running dialogue is the Q and A format, where an entire interview, or almost all of it, is recorded verbatim. Here is a sample from the August 1997 issue of *Runner's World.* Writer Peter Gambaccini interviewed runner and 1966 Olympics star Michael Johnson.

Runner's World: After such an extraordinary 1996 [at the Olympics in Atlanta], how are you going to avoid a psychological letdown in 1997?

Michael Johnson: Everyone asks me that, but from my perspective, it doesn't make sense. This year is more what I'm used to than an Olympic year, so it's back to normal, not a letdown.

The interview continued in this format for two full pages in the magazine.

What is absolutely necessary for all these strategies to work is thorough research and meticulous note taking. No writer yet has found worthy substitutes.

FOR EXAMPLE

A student wrote about how school boards sometimes unwisely sacrifice music education to save money in the budget. While surfing the Internet, he came across an article that he initially thought would be helpful. However, he never used the material for the following reasons:

• The article could not be attributed to a source. No author or sponsoring organization was listed.

• The article was not dated. The only date (10/24/99) was the day the student accessed the article on the Internet. If the article had been published elsewhere, when? How current was the information?

• The article quoted Ernest Boyer and John Ruskin, but never stated where the quotations came from. The footnotes after the names were listed this way on page 2:

2 Boyer, Ernest
3 Ruskin, John

But these references were of no value. Boyer, for example, died in 1995, so the quotation obviously was not from a recent interview. Boyer was one of America's most noted educators. During his lifetime, he wrote several books and dozens of articles and was interviewed and quoted extensively countless times in newspapers, magazines, and professional journals. This statement could be from any of those many works.

President Reagan also was quoted. But the article did not indicate when and where Reagan spoke those words.

The cover story for the August 5, 1999 edition of *Rolling Stone* was titled "All Hat, No Cattle," a revealing profile of George W. Bush by Paul Alexander. According to Alexander, the article was based on interviews with "some 100 people who knew Bush." The article, portions of which are printed here, offers excellent examples of how the interview can provide necessary substance and life to a story. Alexander also demonstrates how paying attention to detail by the writer pays off for the reader.

"All Hat, No Cattle"
by Paul Alexander
(reprinted by permission of Straight Arrow Publishers Company L.P. 1999. All rights reserved)
The forty-sixth governor of Texas was born on July 6th, 1946, in New Haven, Connecticut, where his father, then a young World War II veteran, was rushing through Yale in just two and a half years. By 1948, after George Herbert Walker Bush had graduated Phi Beta Kappa from Yale, he and his wife, Barbara, and their young son moved to Texas, to stake their claim in the oil business. The Bushes would move around some over the next few years before settling in Midland, Texas, a dusty piece of oil patch where George W. passed much of his youth.

In 1953, while Bush was creating Zapata Petroleum with his friends John Overbey and Hugh and Bill Liedtke, Georgie's younger sister, Robin, was diagnosed with leukemia; she died at Memorial Sloan-Kettering Hospital in New York that October. During the months Robin was sick, George and Barbara never revealed her illness to Georgie, then six and attending Sam Houston Elementary

School. Following Robin's death, Georgie tried to ease his mother's grief. "One lovely breezy day, I was in our bedroom when I heard Georgie talking to a neighbor child who wanted him to come over and play," Barbara Bush later wrote in her autobiography. "Georgie said he wanted to, but he couldn't leave his mother. She needed him. That started my cure."

In 1959, after Georgie graduated to San Jacinto Junior High, Bush and his partners split up Zapata, and Bush took its offshore drilling subsidiary. Because he needed to be near the Gulf of Mexico, where Zapata's drilling took place, he relocated his family—by then there were five kids: George, Jeb, Marvin, Neil and Dorothy—to Houston and enrolled Georgie at the Kinkaid School, a private academy favored by Houston's wealthiest families. Two years later, George W. transferred to the Phillips Academy in Andover, Massachusetts, the school his father and grandfather had attended. "He was not a goody-two-shoes," classmate Tom Seligson said, recalling a spring-break trip they took to Fort Lauderdale. "He partied as much as anybody. I don't ever remember him being depressed." Indeed, at Andover, where his nicknames were "Lip" and "Tweeds," Bush was known as an "unexceptional student," as another classmate would later remember, who "played a lot of sports, none of them particularly well." In his senior year, he became head cheerleader.

George W. may not have been as academically inclined as his father, but, according to Tom Craddick, a state representative from Midland who has known the Bushes for years, "George was strong and opinionated, like his mother. She's more of a forceful person than George W.'s father is. George W. says he got his mother's mouth." A prominent Republican is less kind: "Barbara Bush is an exceedingly vindictive, nasty individual with a very high opinion of herself. She's always been that way." Cocky, boisterous, flippant—these were the traits George W. was developing as a young man. They were anathema to his formal father. To crush George W., his father merely had to say he was "disappointed." "Dad was shy," George W. said years later. "We never had 'the talk.' " He never told me to wear a raincoat [condom] or anything. I never had any sense of what his ambitions were for me." But he and his father did have a real affection for each other. "I know George respected his father a lot," says John Kidde, a roommate of George W.'s at Andover. "I remember whenever he greeted his father, he always gave him a hug or grabbed him around the waist."

Despite his modest grades, George W. was accepted at Yale, his father's other alma mater. "He was not accepted because he was a legacy, either," says Henry Chauncey Jr., Bush's adviser at Yale's Davenport College. "It was a time in Yale's history when the admissions office was not being favorable to alumni children, since the school was trying to broaden its base. Some alumni got angry because they didn't think the school was accepting enough legacy students." Clearly, Yale was in transition—and not just concerning admissions. More profound changes were taking place, many of them caused by the Vietnam War. "Yale was on the cusp of change," says Lanny Davis, the former special counsel to Bill Clinton, who was one year ahead of Bush at Yale. "By the end of my time at Yale, there was a light-year of change because of the antiwar and countercultural movements—movements many Yale students joined."

George W. steered clear of the famous anti-war protests there. He majored in history, but he couldn't match his father's Phi Beta Kappa performance. One friend comments that he "didn't set the place on fire" but fell into "that broad middle." Actually, Bush was too busy partying to study. Later, more than one friend would compare him to Otter in *Animal House*. Not only did he join Delta Kappa Epsilon, but he was elected president. Naturally, he wasn't averse to drinking. "Let's just say, liquor was permitted in the fraternity house," says Donald Ensenat, one of Bush's friends at Yale, "and George W. had a good time." Lanny Davis concurs: "We were fraternity brothers, so we went to parties frequently. In all of the times I saw George partying—and we were not known for bashful parties—he was always just drinking and dancing and having lots of fun. I never saw him lose control."

Not surprisingly, Bush had the minor brushes with authority to be expected of a rambunctious frat boy. One Christmas, New Haven police arrested Bush for stealing a wreath from a fraternity house. On another occasion, Princeton University campus police seized Bush along with other Yale students—"all of them well-lubricated," says one eyewitness—when they rushed the football field and tore down the goal posts after Princeton defeated Yale in the Ivy League championship game. "George W. was detained out of the crowd with a few others," Ensenat recalls. "Who knows why they picked him. I have a vivid memory of him walking down the length of the football field with a campus policeman on each side, grabbing him by the arms."

HANDS ON

1. Using the key word(s) from an article topic you are considering, or a new one, consult the Library of Congress Headings to discover related, narrower and broader terms. Search the Internet with those new terms to see if they uncover helpful information not found using the original key word(s).

   - While engaged in the first exercise, note articles or other writings that are not usable because they lack a credible source, contain undated information, or make unsubstantiated claims or generalizations.

2. Select an article topic, preferably one not based solely on your personal experience; choose two persons you might interview in response to the two research questions. Remember, an interviewee can serve a number of purposes: provide general information, overall perspective or background; cite case histories and specific examples; provide anecdotes and personal experiences that illustrate points you want to make.

   - List specific questions you would ask these persons.

   - Seek your teacher's guidance and approval regarding your interviewees and list of questions.

   - Conduct the two interviews, then write a critique of the process. Include in the critique your honest assessment of the various stages of the interview process (selection of the interviewee, scheduling and confirming the interview, writing the questions, and conducting the interview). Answer these questions: Did I come away with what I was seeking from the interviewees? Did I learn more than I had hoped for or planned on? What could I have done differently?

5 Choosing a Title and Writing a Lead

You might think it is too early to think about a title and lead for an article that may not be ready for writing. In fact, you might just be winding up your research. But the reason for choosing a title and lead now is sound. You will need to perfect both before taking the next big step: the query letter to an editor.

The first offerings from you that an editor will judge are the title of your proposed article and the lead sentence(s). If they fail to grab the editor's attention and interest, your article idea may be rejected faster than an editorial assistant can stuff your self-addressed, stamped envelope (SASE) with those familiar but dreaded words, "Your idea does not fit our editorial needs at the present time."

Titles Come in Categories

A title, or headline, should reflect the angle and focus of the proposed article. Just as two writers might approach an idea differently, the title they choose should reflect that difference. For example, two writers propose an article about a new diet. Writer One approaches the idea from the angle of how someone can use and benefit from the diet; she therefore chooses a how-to title. On the other hand, Writer Two wonders whether the marketplace really needs or wants one more diet; he chooses a title that poses just such a question.

Here are some of the more common forms—categories—of titles, with explanations and examples.

How-to.   Goes best with articles that tell the reader how to use a product, perform a task, or construct something. The words "how to" often do not appear in the title, but the intent is obvious.

"Protecting Your Child From Pain" (*Parenting,* May 1999). The article tells a parent "what you can do" about the pain associated with circumcision, burns, and shots.

"Constructing an L-Band Feed Horn" (*Monitoring Times,* April 1999). The article walks the reader through the construction steps, aided by diagrams.

"Put the freeze on air-conditioning bills" (*Woman's Day,* June 1999). The article offers such tips as "use ceiling fans" and "turn off lights when you don't need them."

"36 Ways to Have Fun With Your Hair" (*Mademoiselle,* August 1999). The article tells readers what tools and techniques to use to create such new trends in hair styling as "smooth and slick" and "sexy exits."

Descriptive.   Goes best with articles that want the reader to envision a scene, experience an emotion or sensation, examine an object or collection of objects.

"Home Is Where The Art Is" (*D: Dallas/Fort Worth,* March 1999). The article pictures the work of local artisans who "create pieces that are as practical as they are beautiful."

"scents therapy" (*Mode,* May 1999). The article immediately appeals to the senses: "Stroll the lush gardens of the Ojai Valley Inn and Spa . . . and you'll come across a spritzer bottle cooling on a bed of ice tucked amidst the flowers and greenery."

"New Jersey's million-acre paradox" (*New Jersey Country Roads,* Winter 1999). The article takes the reader into the state's vast Pine Barrens, with its cranberry bogs, rivers stained by pig iron, and little crossroads with such strange names as Ong and Whitesbog.

Question.   Goes best with articles where the writer wants the reader to think about possible answers or perhaps be startled by what the answer might be.

"Child Care: How does your state rate?" (*Working Mother,* August 1999). What mother reading the magazine who places her child in a day care center wouldn't want to know how effective and safe child care is in her state. The reader is forcefully persuaded to read the article by the question.

"Columbine: Whose Fault Is It?" (*Rolling Stone,* May 1999). A very provocative question that most Americans were asking out loud in the wake of the massacre of students in Littleton, Colorado and the rash of other shootings in schools.

"Why invest in the orthopedic industry?" (*Orthopedics Today,* August 1999). The question is addressed to persons in the orthopedic industry who may not be aware that the market is bullish for "76 publicly held musculoskeletel companies."

Statement or Label.   Goes with any article; it is the most common form of title. Frequently however, the title or headline, requires a subhead or lead sentences to fully explain what the article is about.

"journalism.commerce" (*Brill's CONTENT,* August 1999). The meaning of the title is not entirely clear without the following lead sentences: "Web sites are linking information and sales in all sorts of new ways, and it's hard to tell what's what. Can publishers agree on a set of standards to sort it out?"

"Taking Charge" (*Modern Maturity*, January–February 2000). The title is intriguing, but it could mean taking charge of your health or your finances. Even the subheads are not very helpful: "Thinking about reinventing your life? These brave souls stopped thinking and just did it." It is not until the reader gets to the first sentence of the article does he/she discover what the article is all about: "Like all adventures, changing careers requires courage."

"Fighting Fakes" (*The Rotarian*, November 1998). The headline grabs the reader, but again it is necessary to read the subhead to find out what the title refers to: "Product counterfeiting is now a bona fide global racket."

"Fire, Ice, Fossils" (*Natural History*, June 1999). A lead sentence in 24-point bold type explains the meaning of the label: "Born of lava and shifting earth, the glacier-topped Andes hold clues to a continent's past." Now the reader knows what the focus of the article is.

Lead With Your Right Hook

The lead is so named because it denotes the first few sentences or opening paragraph of an article or a query letter to an editor. In a number of printed articles readers may not fully comprehend the meaning of the title (headline) until they read a subhead or lead sentences.

The lead, then, serves two important functions: (1) to help explain the title given an article, or proposed article in the case of a query letter; and (2) to act, in conjunction with the title, as a hook to first grab the editor's attention and, later, a magazine's readers'.

Leads also come in categories, some of them having the same or similar function as titles and others with different functions. Here are the more common leads and how they function.

Anecdote. An anecdote is a very short, self-contained happening (usually one paragraph as a lead) with a beginning and end, and it is one of the more common leads. Its popularity stems from the fact that people like to read about people, particularly if they can identify with the person in the happening. Often, the anecdote is based either on the personal experience of the writer or the experience of someone interviewed by the writer. Occasionally, the anecdote might be based on a third person whose situation bears on the subject matter of the article, or it might be a fictional account (so identified by the writer) to illustrate the main idea or point of the article. Here are a few examples.

"One perfect spring day as I sat on my deck, I looked up from the book I was reading to see my daughter, then 2½, nose-to-nose with the daffodils in our garden. Bending from one flower to another, she gave each of them a gentle kiss. Swamped with love and pride that I had produced such a sweet, tender child, I rushed to sit beside her. That's when she calmly turned, looked me straight in the eye, and said, 'Go away, I don't want you here. I want Daddy.' I was devastated."

This lead begins an article by Margery D. Rosen in the May 1999 issue of *Child* magazine. The article tells parents how to read the real messages behind what Rosen calls "hot button remarks" uttered by children.

"At 9:15 A.M. on Tuesday, October 26, Paul Steiger picked up his office telephone in New York, dialed the general number for the corporate headquarters of Sears, Roebuck and Co. and asked to speak with the company's chairman, Arthur Martinez. It was only 8:15 A.M. in Chicago, but unbeknownst to the switchboard operator, Martinez was already in the building for an early meeting. When the operator couldn't locate the chairman, Steiger left a simple message: Please call Paul Steiger, managing editor of the *The Wall Street Journal*, at this number. . . ."

The article in the February 2000 issue of *Brill's CONTENT* went on to describe how Steiger was trying to advise Martinez that Sears, along with other old, established corporations, had been dropped that morning from the Dow Jones Industrial Average "to make room for younger, hipper stocks."

"On a recent visit to my brother's home, I nervously watched him toss, tussle, flip, swing and tickle his two kids and my own to a point that made me cringe. 'Hey, take it easy!' I finally said. 'Someone's going to get hurt!' My brother poked his head up from under four hysterically laughing kids now intent on 'beating up' their Crazy Uncle Morris. 'Oh, relax,' he answered, somewhat annoyed. 'They're having a great time! I'd never let them get hurt. If you're worried, that's your problem.' "

That's how an article by Grace Bennett about the benefits of rough physical play between children and adults began in the May 1999 issue of *Working Mother*.

You.   Another very popular lead addresses the reader directly. It forces the reader to do one of several things (sometimes all of them at the same time): think, react, or act. The "you" lead is sometimes associated with a how-to article because it may begin telling the reader what to do, but it certainly is not restricted to that category. A word of caution: The "you" lead is usually not effective in a query letter to an editor. The reason, of course, is that, in this instance, the writer is not addressing the audience to whom the lead and article are ultimately directed—magazine readers. Here are a few examples of "you" leads:

"If you're totally ready to go away to college, but are dreading living in a 'traditional/institutional' dorm, don't stress yourself to the breaking point just yet. There are colleges out there with more to offer than cell-block style. One such school is Champlain College, Burlington, VT. They set their students up in restored Victorian-era mansions!"

This lead is from an article by Carla Barletto in the October 1999 issue of *College Bound* magazine.

"To run as well as you possibly can, you need strength in your 'core' muscles—the abdominal and lower-back muscles that attach to your pelvic girdle and spine."

This lead went with a how-to article about exercises a runner can do to strengthen the "core" muscles. The article by Owen Anderson appeared in the August 1997 issue of *Runner's World*.

"If you see a newborn sucking her thumb, you might sigh and think, 'How sweet,' but when your preschooler picks his nose in public, you cringe. Although it may seem to you that your child is the only one biting her nails, twirling her hair, or kicking the table leg, in fact bad habits are incredibly common. Most kids will develop at least one of these behaviors at some point, notes David Arnold, Ph.D., an assistant professor of psychology at the University of Massachusetts Amherst."

Betty S. Wong wrote this lead for her article "The hidden meaning of bad habits," which appeared in the May 1999 issue of *Parents*. This is a good example of a "you" lead that requires readers to think—or rethink—what they have previously believed or assumed. In this case, Wong wants to reassure concerned parents that their child is not the only one who practices bad habits at one time or another in their life.

Descriptive. Like a descriptive title, this category of lead paints a picture. The writer wants the reader to see what he saw, feel what he felt, hear what he heard. Several good "descriptive" leads follow.

"The long blast of the steam whistle did it. That and the rolling start of the four-foot high steel drivers brought the necks craning from the sidewalk, the parking lot and within the passengers' caboose. Good-bye to the balmy air and greening fields of late spring. Destination: Cumbres Pass in the San Juan Mountains and snow so deep it will stop the train."

This lead topped the article "Chama Snow Busting" by Roger Badash in the April 1999 issue of *New Mexico Magazine*. It was a logical selection because the entire article used graphic language to describe the "annual snowdrift-clearing inaugural run of the Cumbres & Toltec Scenic Railroad."

"Most insects that live in cold temperate regions are dormant in winter: carpenter ants hide out in their nests; praying mantises survive the winter as frost-proof eggs. But not honeybees. . . . Pressing together to form a well-insulated cluster the size of a volleyball, and exercising their powerful flight muscles to generate heat, the bees maintain a warm microhabitat inside their hive. Even on winter nights with subzero temperatures, the outermost bees in the cluster rarely cool below 50 [degrees], and those in the center of the cluster experience downright balmy temperatures of 80 [degrees] or more. The fuel for this winter-long heating process is the honey they stockpile inside their hives."

The lead followed this headline and subhead: "Born to Dance: Choreography in a Beehive." The article by Thomas D. Seeley in the June 1999 issue of *Natural History* described in detail how the bees sustain their hive during cold weather.

Question.   What makes a question lead effective, of course, is that the reader is bound to want an answer. The more challenging or tantalizing the question, the more anxious the reader is to get to the answer. In the case of a query letter, a question as lead sentence will hold the editor's attention at least as far as your answer. The following are examples of question leads.

"Should John Adams, Ebbets Field, the sixties, and Tocqueville be knocked off their pedestals? Are Ben Franklin and Bob and Ray far greater than you ever imagined?"

Many readers of the article "Overrated and Underrated" in *American Heritage,* May–June 1999 will keep going just to find out what Ebbets Field is or was and who Tocqueville and Bob and Ray are or were. (Ebbets Field was the home of the Brooklyn—now Los Angeles—Dodgers. Alexis Tocqueville, a French political scientist and historian, gained fame after touring the United States and writing a critique that was at once flattering and faulting. Bob and Ray made radio audiences laugh in the Forties and Fifties.) The article concerned an annual survey of "experts in every field" to find out "what reputation is the most inflated and what's most underappreciated."

"Who's the heat going to drain this summer, you or your bank account? Not much of a choice, is it? But cool doesn't have to come at such a high price. Comfort and cost cutting can go hand in hand if you follow this advice."

A "question" lead, as in this case, can be appropriate for a how-to article. The "advice" referred to in the lead was a series of steps a homeowner can take to save on the cost of air-conditioning. The article by Joseph Woodson Oglesby appeared in the June 1999 issue of *Woman's Day.*

"The great achievement of the past few decades is that we now know everything necessary to grow a business. But will we ever design businesses that grow us?"

This provocative question leads an article titled "The end of the world as we knew it" in the May 1999 issue of *Inc.* magazine. The author, George Gendron, answers that more and more men and women are opting out of the "mainstream economy" and immersing themselves in the "solo economy," a new twist on entrepreneurship.

First Person.   This lead, of course, is a natural one for a personal experience article, but it also can be used to introduce an article, or query, where the writer is simply citing a personal experience, offering an opinion or recalling a reaction in reference to the subject of the article. Here are examples:

"I used to brag that I paid full price for my clothes. It's the truth. While my friends scurried to one-day sales to paw through racks of merchandise, I breezed into my favorite specialty shop, picked out a few ensembles, tried them on and was on my way half an hour later. But the day my co-worker waltzed into the office wearing the same blazer I'd paid nearly twice as much for, I knew reform was imminent. . . ."

This lead went on for another three sentences, an especially long—arguably too long—lead. The point is, however, that the personal experience cited in the lead did not carry over into the article "How To Buy It Faster, Cheaper, Easier" by Betsy Wiesendanger published in the July/August 1999 issue of *Working Mother*. The article was a how-to piece offering readers a series of tips on "ways to slash the cost of nearly everything."

"I am making her sick. Mary Lamielle wants to talk to me outside of her Voorhees home, but she invites me inside as it begins to rain, and that's when the trouble starts. I'm here to learn about a mysterious problem called multiple chemical sensitivity. Now, suddenly, I am the problem."

Here again, the article is not about the personal experience of writer Debra Nussbaum; the first person lead is used only as a connector—an especially effective one—to Nussbaum's research into the causes, symptoms, and manifestations of an unusual malady. The article, which appeared in the *Philadelphia Inquirer*'s Sunday magazine November 14, 1999, contains the experiences of several persons interviewed by Nussbaum who suffer from the same rare ailment.

"Publicly, at least, most rape victims are nameless and faceless, their identities protected by the media to guard their privacy and to avoid additional pain. So after I was raped five years ago in the building where I worked, people were surprised when I allowed my name to be used in media reports. Though I was devastated by the attack, the shame was the rapist's, not mine. My openness was the first sign that I wouldn't conform to the textbook rape-victim profile. The lawsuit was the second."

In this case, the article in the August 1999 issue of *Cosmopolitan* was all about the personal experience of the writer, Lynn Green as told to Joan Ryan.

Surprising.   Sometimes it is desirable to hook an editor or her readers with a lead that may catch them unawares—startle them. Here are several examples of that kind of lead:

"An accurate accounting is always confusing business, so let's just say I robbed a lot of banks. The FBI estimated my total at between 30 and 40. Even I lost count. But I can tell you this: Bank robbery is a major rush. With a serious downside."

Joe Loya recounted his life of crime in an article for the March 1999 issue of *San Francisco* magazine. Imagine if you were a magazine editor receiving a query from Loya that began with those sentences. Even if you eventually turned down the article idea, you would have to know more about Loya and his experience. You would have to read on in the query, perhaps even talk to him on the telephone. The lead is that intriguing.

"The man's voice on the phone got straight to the point. 'I have to reschedule the interview,' he said in a rapid-fire Boston accent. 'Gotta deal with these tigers in New Jersey.' "

The editor or magazine reader does a double take for two reasons: (1) What are tigers doing in New Jersey? and (2) Who is this person who takes care of tigers—a circus trainer, veterinarian, zoo keeper? The article by Beth Baker in the September 1999 issue of *AARP Bulletin* states the man is none of the above; he's John C. Walsh, international projects director for the World Society for the Prevention of Cruelty to Animals.

"Mike Wallace was stunned. The dean of TV investigative reporters— the one who always has a snappy question for every answer—had the gasping look of a man who'd been sucker punched."

Mike Wallace caught off balance? That is a surprise! Exactly the thought D. M. Osborne must have had when he wrote that lead for his article in the July-August issue of *Brill's CONTENT* about the time Wallace's show *60 Minutes* missed a hot story that became the movie The *Insider.*

Straightforward.   Then there's the straightforward lead that tells it like it is—that relies on solid information about the subject of the article to hook the editor in a query or a reader of an article. Here are examples:

"Despite decades of efforts, newsrooms of the nation's newspapers still don't reflect the diversity of the general population, and a recent survey for The Freedom Forum reveals that just hiring more minorities won't close the gap."

Not unexpectedly, the *American Journalism Review* of September 1999 used a news lead on its report of the survey. Newspaper-type leads are appropriate for some magazine articles, particularly, as in this case, when the article is reporting information for the first time, and it is deemed particularly important for the magazine's readers to know.

"In what the American Medical Association (AMA) is terming a historical vote, the group's House of Delegates have decided to form a collective bargaining unit for physicians."

Nothing could be more straightforward than this lead from the August 1999 news magazine *Infectious Diseases in Children.* A similar lead was used to announce the same event in the other medical news magazines published by SLACK. As previously noted, many professions, businesses and the associations to which their members belong publish news magazines, or what Elliot Carlson of *AARP Bulletin* calls magtabs. Straightforward leads are common in these kinds of publications.

"You've probably heard that married people tend to live longer, and recent research indicates that may be true. A large national survey by University of Chicago sociologist Linda J. Waite, Ph.D., found that nearly 90 percent of married women are still alive at age 65, compared to only about 60 percent of divorced or never-married women."

This lead from an article by Sue Ellin Browder in the June 1999 issue of *Woman's Day* reflects the magazine's treatment of a serious, important subject. Even magazines like *Rolling Stone* and *Mademoiselle*, whose articles often dictate spicy titles and leads to match, when they publish articles about such spiceless events as the war in Kosovo and the Columbine massacre (which they did), they choose straightforward leads.

FOR EXAMPLE

It is acceptable—in fact, commonplace—to write leads that combine two or more kinds of leads into one. Here is a combination anecdote-descriptive lead from an article by Gayle Forman in the March 2000 issue of *Seventeen:*

"It's a frigid November night in New York City. Outside the 15th-floor apartment where Diamond, 13, and her mom, Felicia, live, the wind rattles the windows and chases clouds across the Manhattan skyline. But inside things are warm—in every way. Diamond, a tomboyishly beautiful girl with a Noxema complexion, is spending the evening as she usually does, talking, laughing, eating, even dancing—all with her mom. Their conversation meanders from one subject to another; Diamond's day, her schoolwork, guys she's crushing on. Mother and daughter have a tendency to finish each other's sentences, like best friends do."

Dr. Isadore Rosenfeld wrote an article on phlebitis for the January 30, 2000 issue of *Parade* magazine that begins with a straightforward–you combination lead:

"When you have phlebitis, the walls of one or more of your veins are inflamed. The vein can be near the surface of the skin (superficial phlebitis) or somewhere deep inside the body and not visible (deep vein phlebitis). You can have one kind without the other. When the inflammation is accompanied by a clot inside the vein—a frequent occurrence, especially in deep veins—the condition is called thrombophlebitis, and that's potentially serious."

Can you write a lead that will hook an editor and her magazine's readers? Yes. Here are a few examples of excellent leads written by students:

"College is almost upon you. And if you think the battle ends with getting admitted, you're majorly mistaken." (By June Moe Lim for his article published in the October 1999 issue of *College Bound Magazine*.)

"After wrecking my nest, they all flew away! Yes, they have flown the coop and have left me in my wrecked nest with a stranger." (By Faye E. Robinson in her query for an article about how she became reacquainted with her husband after years looking after their children, and how, together, they rebuilt the nest.)

HANDS ON

1. Examine two consumer magazines (paper or online) and identify as many different kinds of leads as you can find.

   - Examine two trade publications (paper or online) and identify as many different kinds of leads as you can find.

2. Select any two leads and rewrite them in a different mode. For example, turn a "how-to" lead into a "question" lead or a "first person" lead into a "you" lead.

   - Select two other leads and combine them into a new lead.

3. Try writing two or more different titles (headlines) for an article idea you have been working on.

   - Try writing two or more different leads for the same or another article idea you have been working on. Which one(s) work best?

6 Writing the Query Letter

A student went for an interview at a local newspaper. While still sitting in his car in the newspaper's parking lot, he discovered he had left at home the folder containing his resume and clippings of articles he had written for other publications. He decided he had two options: (1) go ahead with the interview and apologize to the editor for his forgetfulness, or (2) go home, call the editor and try to reschedule the interview. Not great choices. He picked option one. "The interview was a disaster; I was unprepared and appeared foolish." He didn't get the job.

Whether we like it or not, much of the time we—and our talents—are judged on the basis of first encounters and impressions. Oftentimes, the way we present ourselves the first time is all someone has to go on. They may have no recourse but to evaluate us and our merit on the basis of what they see— in person or in a query letter we send to a busy magazine editor.

Your article idea and you as article writer customarily are offered to an editor in a one-page letter. You are querying—asking—the editor whether he/she is sufficiently interested in the idea and impressed with your writing talent to take a look at the complete article. Most editors prefer receiving a query letter rather than the complete article because they barely have time to read all the letters submitted let alone dozens or hundreds of articles that may vary in length from 250 to 2,500 words.

Editors are inundated with article ideas, many of them foolish and completely inappropriate for the magazine to which they have been submitted.

"Do you know how much junk mail an editor sees . . . ?" Michael J. Bugeja asked in his book *Guide to Writing Magazine Nonfiction* (Allyn & Bacon, 1998). "At some mass magazines, such as *Cosmopolitan*, thousands of pieces each month. And, of course, much of it is inappropriate: articles on onionskin, crumpling like gift wrapping out of the envelope; tomes about the Spanish American War sent to a women's magazine whose readers are concerned about beauty, health, fashion, travel, careers, horoscopes, and romance; psycho-fiction (or worse, nonfiction) describing in detail what the sicko is going to do to the editor if she rejects him one more time; essays from prisoners claiming "I didn't do it" and seeking—what else?—pen pals; postcards from good Christian God-fearing Daughters of the American Revolution obsessing over the whereabouts of grandmother's memoir, sent to the editor with a SASE [self-addressed, stamped envelope] or an explanation; and much, much more."

What Editors Say

A group of magazine editors was asked what, in their view, is the "single most important element in an article query." This is what they replied:

- "Get to the point quickly." (Roberta Redford, publisher/editor of *Contemporary Songwriter.*)
- "Tell us *why* the readers of our special-interest magazine should/would/need to read this article." (Jon C. Halter, editor of *Scouting.*)
- "[Tell] how the story executes the mission of my publication." (Whitney Wood, managing editor of *NurseWeek* and *HealthWeek.*)
- "[Tell] why the story belongs in my magazine." (Julia Bencomo Lobaco, editor of *Vista.*)
- "Evidence that the author understands the audience s/he wishes to write for." (Tom Bowden, managing editor of *Tech Directions.*)
- "A succinct, evocative, to-the-point, one-two punch!" (Lesley S. Abravanel, managing editor of *Porthole Cruise.*)
- "The writer needs to show they understand our audience and what is important to them." (David Hein, executive editor of *Christian Century.*)
- "Lead in with an outstanding segment of writing. Not only does such an approach adequately enlighten us to your topic, it illustrates your ability to write, engage a reader, and entertain!" (Gina LaGuardia, editor-in-chief of *College Bound.*)
- "Knowledge of the market. We're a trade magazine for retailers. When I get a query talking about how important the article is for teachers (instead of school supply retailers), then I realize the writer does not know our market." (Tina Manzer, editorial director of *Educational Dealer, edplay, Games Retailer,* and *Arts Materials Retailer.*)
- "A fully developed idea of what the article will present." (Tom Hamilton, editor of *Balloon Life.*)
- "Why is the topic unique? In what way will it enlighten the reader?" (Susan Kostrzwa, managing editor of *Specialty Travel Index.*)

Based on the responses of these editors, the advice of other editors, and the experience of students and professional writers, the following tips can guide you in the preparation of query letters to magazines:

Tip One: Know the magazine

Editors believe they receive so many inappropriate queries for the following reasons:

1. A writer, inexperienced but nevertheless bold, wants to hit it big first time out and, therefore, submits queries to magazines with the highest circulation and that pay very well (perhaps in reverse order). For example, a query about the same idea and presented the same way may go to *Reader's Digest, Cosmopolitan, Parade,* and *Rolling Stone.*

2. A writer sends out the same article idea to a large number of diverse publications, most of which the writer is not familiar with, hoping that the scatter shot approach will—strictly by luck—hit a right target.

3. A writer, using a directory such as *Writer's Market,* believes it is enough to rely on the book's description of a magazine, that it is not necessary to actually read the publication. Of course, the editors of *Writers Market* would be the first to say there is no substitute for examining one or more issues of a magazine for which you wish to write.

Much information can be gleaned by examining two or three issues of a publication. You find answers to your questions:

• About the kinds of articles the editor regularly selects for publication. For example: Mostly how-to? A lot of personal experience accounts? In-depth and detailed, or short and limited in scope?

• About writing style preferred by the editor and the magazine's readers. For example: Conversational and bright (hip) or more formal? Leads primarily of one kind—anecdote, you—or varied? Reading level? (Apply the Gunning Fog Index.)

• About reader demographics and preferences (check out ads in addition to editorial content). For example: age, gender, income level, lifestyle, work experience or career field, political persuasion?

Tip Two: Remember, you're writing a business letter

The query letter, first of all, is a business letter, single spaced and containing the standard elements of a business letter (see sample letters in the **For Example** section). Always send your letter to an editor by name, not just "editor" and never, never "to whom it may concern." Names of appropriate editors are available in at least three locations: in the masthead of their publication and in such directories as *Writer's Market* and *Bacon's Magazine*

Directory. Appropriate editors usually have the title of editor or editor-in-chief. If your article idea fits one of the magazine's departments, send your letter to the editor of the proper department. Sometimes, a magazine will ask writers to send query letters to a designated editorial assistant or articles editor. If no other editors are listed, it is all right to send your letter to the managing editor. In most publications, however, the managing editor is primarily in charge of production rather than editorial content.

Address the editor in the salutation by his or her last name, unless you know the editor personally. I have had to return letters to students who addressed an editor by his or her first name. Aesop's warning that "familiarity breeds contempt" may apply in this instance.

Tip Three: Structure your letter

A standard query letter is one page; editors usually can't or won't take the time to go further. The letter divides roughly into these parts and in this order:

Lead paragraph.   A good lead—the hook—either grabs the interest and attention of an editor or, if it is poorly conceived and written, allows the editor to get away and sentences your idea to an untimely rejection.

Summary and explanatory paragraphs.   This is a one-page letter, so keep paragraphs short. Here is where you summarize your idea and tell the editor how you expect to develop it. Also, describe the research you have conducted and/or what research you expect to undertake. Consider the following leads and summary/explanatory paragraphs from actual query letters:

Lead

She dropped out of high school when the first of her three children was born 17 years ago, but now Rowanna Saxton aspires to law school. It is a nearly impossible dream—but so was earning a high school equivalency or G.E.D. diploma at age 31, and she accomplished that goal last September.

Summary/explanatory paragraphs

Saxton attends the Family Developmental Center in Baltimore. She is one of dozens of women—mostly black, poor and in their twenties or thirties—who dropped out of school when they gave birth. They want to earn their G.E.D. so they can get a better job or go on to college.

Last year, 67% of the women who took the G.E.D. test passed it.

Lead

"Down in southern New Jersey, they make glass. By day and night, the fires burn on in Millville and bid the sand let in the light." Carl Sandburg wrote those lines 88 years ago. They still make glass down in Millville. In fact, they blew the world's largest bottle—175 gallons and eight feet tall—at Wheaton Village just last month.

Summary/explanatory paragraphs

Wheaton Village is not far from Alloway, where Caspar Wistar and a team of glass blowers from Europe introduced glass making to America in the early 1700s. Today, Wheaton Village (named for the founder of the Wheaton Glass works in 1888) boasts one of the world's great museums, featuring 20,000 square feet of glass objets d'art, from a Wistarburgh jar to rare Tiffany vases.

It is also one of the few places left in the country where visitors not only can watch master glass blowers still plying their craft, but where they can design and make their own paperweight in the reconstructed glass factory.

Lead

So, I asked myself the other day, what's Al Blaustein been up to lately.

Summary/explanatory paragraphs

And Al said on the phone that he had recently met with a representative from the Republic of Russia about drafting a separate constitution for that rebellious province, and, oh yes, Saud Al-Sabah, Kuwait ambassador to the United States, talked to him about possible moves toward democracy in that country once the Iraqis are driven out. Then there was that trip to Japan to advise the government about possible implications of modifying Article 9 in their constitution, the part that prevents them from sending armed forces to the Persian Gulf or anywhere else.

Albert P. Blaustein, who has never taught constitutional law in 35 years as a professor at Rutgers University Law School, has been writing constitutions and advising governments on constitutional law around the world since 1967. The modern constitutions of Fiji and Liberia are among those that bear his imprint.

Lead

What are the ten most important questions your readers should ask their child's school administrators, and what are the ten most critical observations they should make?

Summary/explanatory paragraphs

I know the answers. From 700 elementary school principals I surveyed, as well as a group of parents and community activists I interviewed.

The question ranked number one: What is the classroom–teacher ratio? (It should be approximately 1–18 in the elementary grades.) The key observation: Do students appear to be actively involved in learning?

The survey was conducted with the assistance of the National Association of Elementary School Principals.

Paragraph about your qualifications as writer.   At this point in the letter, you should tell the editor about your experience as a writer and why you should be the one to write this particular article. You might, for example, briefly describe articles you have written that appeared in other publications.

These might include your college newspaper and magazine or a local weekly and daily newspaper. You also should indicate that clippings from this body of work are enclosed. Naturally, select only your best work.

Refer to any particular background or knowledge that makes you especially qualified to write the proposed article. Perhaps you grew up in a city and know first hand about single mothers who struggle to further their education or obtain a better job. Maybe you spent a couple of Saturdays at Wheaton Village learning how to blow glass. Let's say you want to write an article about the hard-sell marketing strategies hospitals use today as health care becomes more competitive. The fact that you completed courses in public relations and advertising would be important to mention. Suppose your idea is a how-to article describing what parents should look for in a preschool for their child. If you work(ed) part-time at such a school, you should point out how your experience will complement suggestions from other credible sources.

Most students currently enrolled in a class on magazine article writing indicate their status in a query letter. However, there are the proverbial two schools of thought on the wisdom of stating that fact:

School 1: An editor notes that you are a student of magazine article writing and finds that a plus. Presumably, you are learning skills that will ensure that your work will at least be more polished than that of someone who is untutored.

School 2: An editor notes that you are a student of magazine article writing and decides not to take a chance on you because you are still learning what to do.

Alas, we have no reliable information to suggest which school is most accurate.

Paragraph about available photos and suggested art.   If your proposed article would be enhanced by pictures, drawings, graphs, charts, cartoons, or maps, so advise the editor. You do not necessarily have to be the one to supply the art work. For example, suppose your article describes a tour—Victorian homes in the region where you live, "cool" clubs at a famous resort—and a map showing routes connecting the places would help the reader. The editor might appreciate your suggestion and descriptions, but the editor would assign a graphics artist to actually draw the map.

On the other hand, if you have access to professional quality color slides (transparencies) or other appropriate photos, describe what you have. In some cases, if you have particularly good photos and they are especially important to readers' appreciation of your article, send one or two along with your query letter. If you do, make sure they are duplicates. Keep the originals.

If you plan to take photos or have them taken, or if you are making arrangements for graphs, drawings, etc., so advise the editor, but briefly. Chapter Nine goes into more detail about photographs and other art work.

What NOT to include in your query letter.   Be forewarned that the first two of the following three suggestions are arguable. Read them over, suggest discussing them in class with your teacher and colleagues; quiz a couple of editors for their reaction.

1. Do not begin your query letter by asking the editor, "Would you be interested in an article about_____?" For one thing, it invites the harried editor to respond too quickly: "No." Primarily, however, it is a lame start to a query that you hope will convince the editor to purchase your article.

2. Do not suggest a length for your article. Many editors are put off by writers, particularly those with little experience, who suggest a feature article of 1,500 to 2,500 words. First of all, many magazines contain few articles of that length, and, secondly, it is likely that most such features are contributed by staff writers or assigned to experienced writers whose work the editor is familiar with. A number of editors advise writers with the least experience to initially submit article ideas for magazine departments where the average length may run from 500 words up to 1,000.

The point, however, is that the editor will advise you how many words your article should be. If an editor initially interested in your idea has in mind a 750-word article and you propose in your query letter an article double that length, you may have killed a sale.

3. Do not flatter yourself or call undue (and probably unearned) attention to your talent. Editors are not impressed, and are in fact turned off by such sentences as these: "I have been told that I have a special knack for dialogue." "The editor of the local daily said my article on dormitory life was one of the best pieces he's seen in a long time." "You can be assured I will turn in an article that is both very informative and highly entertaining." Your work will speak for itself.

Tip Four: You may submit the same idea to more than one publication

Simultaneous submissions are acceptable, but keep these points in mind:

- Avoid the random, shotgun approach. You may want to send your one idea to two or three publications that you have determined in advance are appropriate markets, but do not scatter your idea to a half dozen magazines, several of which you are only guessing as to their appropriateness.

- Be prepared to go with the first acceptance (if there is one). Suppose you send your idea to three publications, but you have your heart set on only one. Your idea is accepted quickly by one of the other publications, and the editor asks you to send the article as soon as possible. Do you hold out for the magazine you prefer? Probably not a good decision. Rejections are plentiful; acceptances are rare.

• Since most publications buy first time rights or all rights to publish your article, you cannot sell the same article to two or more similar (and perhaps competitive) publications.

Tip Five: Think of different angles and markets for the same idea

This suggestion may sound like a contradiction of Tip Four, but it is not. The difference is that, in this case, the same article idea expressed in pretty much the same way is not being submitted to similar kinds of publications. Now, you create new angles and different approaches to the same idea and send them to dissimilar publications.

For example, suppose you are familiar with a band that has discovered a new sound by blending guitar chords with music made by a harpsichord. First of all, you might vary your idea angle and query letter slightly for two different consumer publications: *Guitar Magazine* and *Keyboard Magazine.* Then, you might rewrite the idea and query letter again for a trade magazine such as *Guitar Shop,* which circulates among guitar dealers.

Several years ago, the *Journal of Telecommunications in Higher Education* was looking for articles reporting how colleges and universities were financing their development of distance learning, interactive television, and other electronic learning systems. The *Journal* is the official magazine of the Association of College & University Telecommunications Administrators. I wrote a query letter to the *Journal* outlining efforts New Jersey was making to underwrite the costs of a rapidly expanding network. The *Journal* bought and published the proposed article.

Shortly thereafter I sent a query letter to *New Jersey Monthly* that began as follows: "New Jersey may be less than two years away from linking most of its 563 public school districts, 46 colleges and universities, and dozens of libraries in a giant cybercampus featuring distance learning, interactive television, teleconferencing and Internet." The magazine did not accept the proposal, but the approach was sound. I had spent a great amount of time in research (including a number of interviews) for the *Journal* article. It made sense to recycle the research findings (some of which did not fit the *Journal* piece) in a different market.

Angela Adair-Hoy, publisher of *WritersWeekly.com,* reported in her August 1999 online newsletter: "Last month . . . I submitted 20 queries in about an hour by e-mail. . . . The query topic was the same, yet targeted to each publication's audience (for example, interviewing online office supply firms for an office supply magazine; interviewing online computer firms for a computer magazine). I changed two essential words in the query letter, added each editor's name, and hit send. Much to my surprise, I received a $300 assignment in less than an hour. A week later, I received another $300 assignment, and this week (almost a month later) I received a $500 assignment. These assignments all resulted from the same query letter." Adair-Hoy's advice to her newsletter's subscribers: If you have one good article idea and one good query letter, take a second and third look at it. "Refocus, reslant, and 'reprint' it for other magazines. A good query can go a long way!"

Querying Online

You no doubt noticed in the previous paragraph that Angela Adair-Hoy stated she sent 20 queries by e-mail. Not letters through the U.S. Postal Service. Many magazines today accept e-mail queries, and both *Writer's Market* and *Bacon's Magazine Directory* now list the e-mail address for most publications.

Some magazines in their directory listing will specify the method they prefer writers use to query the editor, or they may give the writer options. For example, in *Writer's Market 2000*, the editors of *National Geographic* specify that writers are to query by mail. On the other hand, in the same directory and on the same page, the editors of *Hope* magazine state: "Accepts queries by mail, e-mail, fax."

As you would suspect, online magazines and online versions of paper magazines normally prefer to have writers query via e-mail.

The contents of your query letter remain essentially the same regardless of the method you use to transmit it to an editor.

An Important Postscript

Every query letter should include as an enclosure a self-addressed and stamped return envelope (SASE). Remember, most magazines have a very small staff, and the profit margin is stretched mighty thin. For at least those two reasons, editors will rarely take the time and go to the expense of responding to every query by typing the writer's address on an envelope and affixing a stamp. Especially if the response is a rejection, which, of course, it most often is.

In order to include a standard size (#10) SASE along with your query letter, you should plan to use a larger envelope (#12 legal size) to send to the editor. A number of students have reported difficulty in preparing these envelopes because typewriters are an endangered species on most campuses. Also, they often do not have easy access to a computer/printer that will handle just two envelopes. What many have done in such a circumstance is to print labels for the envelope to the editor and the SASE. However, we advise against the use of labels. Think of the mail you've received with a label on the envelope instead of your name typed. Isn't your first reaction that this is junk mail, or at least from someone who is scattering the very same message among a number of persons more or less selected at random?

What's the answer? Find a typewriter somewhere. Perhaps in a secretary's office on campus. As a last resort, if your handwriting is especially legible, you may write the name of the editor and magazine address on the outside envelope and your name and address on the SASE. It's better than a label.

FOR EXAMPLE

Kimberly Tweed was a junior at Rowan University in Glassboro, New Jersey in the fall of 1998 when she enrolled in a magazine article writing course. In December of that year, as an assignment for the course, she wrote a query letter to Gina LaGuardia, editor-in-chief of *College Bound* magazine. The letter read as follows:

> Dear Ms. LaGuardia:
>
> You're so busy with applications, SATs, and visits that you may be missing out on one important aspect of your college life. Where are you going to live? For many students the only choice is dorm life, but for others that decision is not so easily made. Some of us are presented with the option of driving to and from class from some point other than a dorm room.
>
> There are many things to consider before becoming a commuter student. There are also many things you need to prepare yourself for after the decision is made. Often, schools take so much time telling you about life on campus that the students who don't live there are left lost. Hopefully, my article will give the insight needed in deciding whether or not to become a mobile student and also a how-to on doing it the right way. In my article I will explain the pros and cons of life as a commuter student and also list ways to make the experience better for anyone who decides to commute to school.
>
> I am currently a junior at Rowan University in Glassboro, New Jersey. I have driven to and from my classes for almost three years now. This and my current studies in Journalism give me the experience needed to write such an article. If necessary, it is possible for me to provide photos with my article.
>
> Thank you for your consideration.

LaGuardia responded that Tweed's article idea did not fit into the magazine's schedule at that time, but that her query letter would be kept on file for future consideration. This is not an unusual response from an editor. It is not a rejection. "In fact, the writer should be encouraged," said LaGuardia when asked to talk about what happened between the time she received Tweed's query and the publication of Tweed's article in the January/February 2000 issue of the magazine.

"First of all, like most magazines, we have a huge lead time [between the time an article is accepted and its publication]," said LaGuardia. "In our case it is at least four to five months. Also, from time to time, we get behind in queries." This also is not unusual, for two reasons:

1. Most magazine staffs are very small, so an editor is often required to take on a number of duties at the same time: read query letters, respond to query letters, edit articles for the next issue, work with writers on articles for upcoming issues, proof copy, plan future issues, answer phone calls, and meet with staff members and others. And that's not necessarily all of the duties.

2. Editors may receive more query letters in a week than most of us receive junk mail in a year. Because of this fact and the other duties enumerated in reason one, an editor may be weeks or months responding to a query. In fact, most magazine entries in *Writer's Market 2000* advise writers they should not expect to receive a response to queries for at least one month. A number of publications say two or more months.

When LaGuardia was able to get back to Tweed's query, she decided that Tweed's personal experience as a commuter constituted only part of the story concerning college students' living arrangements. "We concluded that commuting is only one of three possibilities," said LaGuardia. The other two are campus dormitory and off-campus housing. "We like to encourage writers and work with them, so we went back to Kimberly and suggested she expand on her original idea. She did as we asked. She was great!"

Tweed remembers very well how long it took before she heard from LaGuardia. "I sent the letter in December," she said, "and I didn't hear anything until early the next summer. I had about given up hope." Working with LaGuardia was a good learning experience, said Tweed. "I pretty much followed her suggestions and interviewed other students with different experiences from mine. The result was a better article. When it was published, the article was shorter than how I'd written it, but I learned that you don't necessarily get what you thought you wanted in the first place."

Here is Tweed's article as it appeared in print more than a year after she submitted her query letter:

"Hang Your College Hat"
by Kimberly Tweed
College Bound Magazine, *January/February 2000*
(Reprinted by permission of Ramholtz Publishing, Inc.,
www.collegebound.net)
Here you are—a short time from the end of your life as you've known it for the past 17 or 18 years. You've probably already taken the SATs, sent out your applications, and settled back to wait for those acceptance letters to start rolling in.

The way you see it, pretty soon you'll be packing your bags and heading off to the dorm.

Before you buy the perfect pair of shower shoes, however, think about the huge decision you'll soon be making—where you'll live while attending college. This is an important and multifaceted decision, one you'll want to take some quality time to ponder.

What will be the best for you? How does each living arrangement factor into your financial concerns? Where will you be content and successful as a student?

Depending on if you dorm, reside off campus, or stay at home and commute, it's important that you think about the pros and cons of spending a thousand bucks on the college meal plan, frequenting furniture stores in addition to study hall, or settling in for another four years with the folks.

The Dynamics of Dorm Life

"Living in the dorm gives you a sense of what college is really like," says Shaun Yates, who spent two years dorming at Middle Georgia College, Cochran, GA. "I think you end up missing out on a lot if you never live on campus. [Being there] gives you the chance to maintain your own space for the first time. It really gives you your first look at adulthood." This is a popular notion among many students and parents. To many, college just isn't college unless you live in a dorm.

Dorm life is great in that way. You and your roommate get your own space and are asked for the first time to be completely responsible for yourselves. You have to get to class on your own, make it to the dining hall within designated hours, wash your clothes, and keep up with your schoolwork with no reminders from anyone. You are also in close proximity to teachers for extra help, clubs and organizations, and other students who are in the same boat as you.

Living on campus, however, can become a struggle in other ways. Many feel the pressure of constantly being faced with school and having no place to escape. And then, there's the whole different-lifestyle dilemma amongst roommates.

"Freshman year, I lived in an all-girls, all-freshman dorm," says Sarah Walters, who now lives off campus while attending Ohio University, Athens, OH. "I came from out of state and there was a major culture clash between my roommate and I. It's weird adjusting to dorm life; you never know who you are going to end up with."

That means you may be faced with a *Felicity*esque roomie or become a less than ideal dorm-dweller yourself. If you're the type who may become so consumed with dorm parties that you'll lose sight of why you came to college in the first place, develop a balanced work/play game-plan ahead of time.

The World in Between

When searching for a world in between campus and home, especially one that offers both sides of the collegiate coin, many students choose to live off campus. In fact, most of the areas surrounding colleges and universities have housing units specifically available to students.

"I never had the choice of being able to live on campus—the school didn't have room for all the freshmen in the dorms," explains Lauren Sullivan, a junior at Penn State University, State College, PA, who's happy with her off-campus abode.

"You definitely grow up faster because you're not babied like you are in the dorms," she says. "No one comes and puts toilet paper in my bathroom when it runs out, no one washes my windows or vacuums my hallway."

For many students, such on-their-own living does wonders for strengthening their responsibility-GPA. "I think I am a lot more mature than I would be if I had lived in the dorms," Lauren continues. "I was forced to live on my own as soon as I left home."

It's hard to say if the choice to live off campus in your own place is actually cheaper than dorming. For one, you'll have a bunch of expenses like phone, cable, and electricity that you'll have to pay for separately, as opposed to having them all combined on your dorm bill—this makes it sometimes hard to compare.

The thing about dorms, too, is that no matter how many roomies you have, you always pay the same price. If you grab a place off campus and split all the expenses evenly, however, you may be able to cut your costs dramatically. An $800 apartment including utilities can become a $200 apartment with utilities if you room with three others.

Of course, don't forget about the lease agreements many off-campus apartment landlords require. Have a plan for what you'll do with your pad on breaks and during the summer. You'll have to pay rent, whether or not school's in session.

The Commuter Connection

The third dwelling choice many students make—living at home and commuting to college—is usually done because of finances.

According to writer Shen Eng, in a recent article she contributed to Quicken Online, "Skyrocketing College Costs: Advice for Cash-Strapped Parents," the price of college tuition, room, board, and meals averages between $14,000 for public and $31,000 for private institutions each year.

With a bill like that, the savings for students who opt to live at home and travel to school are extremely beneficial.

"I lived on campus for two years and have since moved home," says Kim Washart, a junior at Rowan University, Glassboro, NJ. "I lived in the dorms for the experience, then moved home to save money. A 15-minute commute is worth the money I am saving."

The price of dealing with your parents and living by the same rules you had in high school, however, is a cause of concern for some commuter students.

"I definitely have a lot less freedom than I did before," says Kristin Kennedy, who attends Atlantic Cape Community College, Mays Landing, NJ, and is back at home now after a year away at school.

"Today I had a ton of work and had to stop and run out to the store to pick up cold cuts for my dad." Not being able to get away with the things you can at school can be frustrating, too, she explains. "I heard about it for a week when I missed a class that I was just too tired to go to and knew was unimportant," Kristin recalls.

For some students who hop in the car to jet home or to a part-time job right after classes, there's the common worry that an integral part of the college experience is being missed.

Kristin agrees: "I am never involved with school activities. I may hear about a party or concert while I'm there, but I don't belong to any clubs. I work every day that I am not on campus."

Kim, on the other hand, says, "I really do stay involved even with the commute and my part-time job. I still party here and am involved with activities, so I don't feel like I am missing out. I know a lot of people and have a lot of friends here."

Speaking of long counts between sending a query letter and getting the article published, how about nearly two years? TL Enterprises in California publishes *Trailer Life* and *Motor Home.* Both magazines serve the growing number of families who own recreational vehicles (RVs). I had an article published in *Trailer Life* in 1994. In February 1995, I had an idea for another article, and submitted it to Barbara Leonard, then and still five years later, editorial director.

It is important to note here that a writer is likely to receive a more attentive reading of his query letter from an editor who has published the writer's work before. Once your work has been accepted the first time, you are a better known quantity. The editor feels she can depend on you in these ways:

- coming up with an idea suitable for her magazine's readers
- researching thoroughly
- writing well enough the first time so the article will not require extensive rewriting
- submitting the final article on time

Thus, the query letter sent Barbara Leonard in February 1995 began by reminding her of the previous article. Also, the salutation used her first name because of previous contacts by letter and telephone. Notice the references to research, an important ingredient in any query letter, but particularly in one proposing an article based on or recording historical events.

Dear Barbara:

I'm on the trail again ("Coastal Heritage Trail," *TL* June 1994). This time I am proposing a piece titled "Following the Patriots." Within a 35-mile radius of Philadelphia's Independence Hall are the sites of turning-point battles in the American Revolution.

Trenton, NJ: On Christmas Day, 1776, the defeated and dejected Continental Army scored the Army's first victory here. "The patriot cause, which had seemed desperate, now took on new life, and hope," wrote eminent historian Henry Steele Commanger.

Princeton, NJ: After Trenton, the Americans chased the British out of western New Jersey by defeating them here. The win "had an incalculable effect in restoring the shattered patriot morale," wrote Commanger.

Chadds Ford, PA: Less than a year later, the patriot cause was in trouble again. Washington's Army tried in vain to prevent the British from occupying Philadelphia in September, 1777. The battle on the banks of the Brandywine River here resulted in 700 Americans being killed or wounded, one of the Army's worst losses of the war.

Monmouth, NJ: The British spent the winter of 1777–78 partying in Philadelphia, while the Americans died by the score at nearby Valley Forge. Come the spring, the British abandoned the city and Washington's rag-tag followed them north into New Jersey. Here, the Americans attacked the British rear guard. When the entire army turned to face the small American force, Washington rode up and down the line, thereby narrowly avoiding a rout. His heroics ensured another day for his army and a future for the nation.

Battlefield parks now mark the sites of these crucial events in our history, and there is much to see. All battlefields can be reached by major roads.

Cordially,

Barbara Leonard responded to the query on March 3. Her letter was short and to the point:

Thanks for your recent query. We'd be happy to consider your suggested article on speculation. Please make it about 1,500 words and include a strong RV focus, good 35 mm slides of RVs and scenery.

Best regards,

As Kimberly Tweed also discovered, editors prefer to determine the length of articles. What happened to the article after it was accepted is not atypical. It was scheduled twice to run in *Trailer Life* and then cut close to deadline when advertising dictated fewer number of pages in those two issues. Finally, the article was shifted from *Trailer Life* to *Motor Home*, probably because the RV seen in the transparencies submitted with the article showed a motorized RV as opposed to an RV pulled by another vehicle. *Motor Home* finally published the article in its January 1997 issue.

Following are several query letters to magazine editors written by students of magazine article writing. In each case a critique is offered. You are invited to critique as well, keeping in mind the various tips described in this chapter. Only the names of the editor to whom the letter was directed and the student have been omitted.

The first letter is addressed to the editor of *Hope Magazine*. The magazine is described in *Writer's Market 2000* as follows: "Quarterly magazine covering humanity at its best and worst. 'We strive to evoke empathy among readers.' "

Letter One
Dear Editor:

Generosity is rarely in short supply around the holidays, and food banks often benefit through abundant donations. Frozen turkeys and canned cranberries cram the shelves at pantries across the country as the spirit of giving infects families caught up in Thanksgiving and Christmas preparations. However, what happens to those public cupboards once their donors have forced the last mouthful of chestnut stuffing and vacuumed up the last stubborn, scraggly pine needles?

Many food banks are commonly faced with shortages, especially of such staples as pasta, cereal, and tuna, especially during those months between Christmas and Thanksgiving.

As such, I propose a 1,000 to 1,500-word article illustrating the crisis and demonstrating how such deficiencies provide a charitable venue for those *Hope Magazine* readers looking for ways to make a difference and make life better for others—and aren't they all? After providing personal accounts of the importance of food banks from those who staff them and those who patronize them, I will explain the needs of these charities that cater to the most basic human need. I will also offer simple ways for readers to help alleviate the shortages; for example, when purchasing staple items for your own household, pick up an extra donation to your local food bank.

Such a topic is especially timely considering the staggering number of hungry children in a nation of such staggering wealth. Furthermore, recent welfare reform measures have left many needy families without the benefit of food stamps and, therefore, without enough food.

Thank you for your consideration, and I look forward to hearing from you.
Sincerely
P.S. I can furnish accompanying pictures.

Critique. The writer effectively uses a question lead to prompt the editor to look to the next paragraph for the answer. The second and third paragraphs provide a clear and sufficiently detailed explanation of how the writer plans to develop the article. In the third paragraph, the writer smartly addresses the editor's concern that articles "evoke empathy among readers."

Writer's Market 2000 reported that articles in *Hope Magazine* run between 250 and 4,000 words, a very wide spread indeed. The writer here has proposed an article length of 1,000 to 1,500 words. If the suggestion is based on the average length of most feature articles in the magazine as noted by the writer after scanning several issues of the publication, the proposal might be merited. However, you are advised against giving a word count, especially if you have arrived at the number either by making a wild guess or because the magazine pays more for longer articles.

The fourth paragraph provides two excellent reasons why the article would be timely, even considering the long lead time between article acceptance and publication.

The writer has offered no personal information. As previously pointed out, whether or not to refer to your status as a student of magazine article writing is debatable. However, in this instance the absence of any mention of experience may work against the writer.

Using a postscript to call attention to photo availability is not a bad idea. Sometimes a postscript set apart will get closer scrutiny than if the same information was contained in the body of the letter.

The writer has not indicated the SASE as an enclosure.

Letter Two
Dear Editor:

The frequent misuse of over-the-counter drugs has, and most likely, will always exist, due to their accessibility, and the consumer's ignorance to understand the effects of the drug. In a similar market, the same problems are being experienced with legal performance enhancing drugs, at an alarming rate.

Legal performance enhancing drugs (PEDs), such as those taken by St. Louis Cardinals slugger Mark McGwire, who broke Roger Maris's single-season home run record in 1998, can be purchased over-the-counter, just as easily as one could purchase Tylenol or vitamins.

I propose to write an article which will briefly describe a few different kinds of PEDs that are available to the consumer market, their purpose and functions, and how they can be taken to be most effective. My primary concern will be to make the reader aware of the risks, of taking these drugs improperly. I will also address the common misconception of synthetic PEDs, in comparison to their herbal counterparts.

The article will consist of actual instances where consumers have taken PEDs improperly, and have suffered many complications resulting in such complications as liver failure, causing eventual death. I will also include a personal testimony, describing my experience with PEDs, and how they positively and negatively effected me.

I am a college student that has had experience as and with, many athletes at a college level, who have, are currently, or plan on using PEDs to increase their physical performance. I hope to create an awareness of the obvious benefits, but most importantly, the potential dangers of using these drugs.

Thank you for your consideration.

Sincerely,

Critique. To begin, this is a very poorly written letter. The writer doesn't know where to place commas, and the opening sentences of the last two paragraphs are atrocious. However, the real problem with this query is that it was written at all—and especially to *Better Health* magazine. The entry for the magazine in *Writer's Market 2000* states, "Prefers to work with published/ established writers." That doesn't mean the editors will not consider queries from new writers, but it does imply that, when it comes to articles about "wellness/prevention issues," the editors would rather rely on writers whose experience is most likely to ensure accurate and carefully researched reporting. It is unlikely that the editors would turn to a college student for a sensitive article probing and exposing the dangers of performance enhancing drugs.

Also, the query is not well-focused. The writer talks about both the benefits and dangers of PEDs, and the editor might fear the writer might submit one of those school papers that presents both sides of an issue and never makes a strong argument for either point of view.

Letter Three
Dear Editor,

Frequently overlooked for the more accessible south, England's most northerly country has much to offer the traveler desiring open spaces full of natural beauty. It is a land full of history and heritage that dates back to ancient times. One can expect to see cathedrals, castles, country houses, museums and gardens set amidst some of the most spectacular scenery that Britain has to offer. There are many adventures in store here for the person who truly desires to experience cultural enlightenment.

I would like to write an article for your magazine based on my four month experience studying abroad in Newcastle-upon-Tyne. During my time at University in England, I took courses that had a strong focus on British culture. With members of the historical society there, I visited a myriad of significant places associated with some of the country's most important historical periods. I am also an amateur photographer and have a complete pictorial record of my journey that would complement the article nicely.

Sincerely,

Critique.   Travel magazines want articles with a very narrow focus—a specific angle. For example, such a magazine might entertain an article on the thrills and scares of descending into the Grand Canyon on a mule, but not be at all interested in a piece about "the Grand Canyon." The problem with this query is that the writer does not make clear what the article's focus would be other than "British culture." The editor might fear the writer would pass a mighty brush stroke over every castle, cathedral, and museum in northern England without ever offering a closeup picture of any one site.

The writer at least gives the editor reason to believe she has done more than merely sampled British culture as an ordinary tourist might. She studied it with the eye and ear of a scholar. Editors are usually and rightly impressed by a writer's knowledge of and expertise in the subject he or she wants to write about.

It is a plus that the writer has pictures to illustrate the article, but she dampens the editor's enthusiasm for them by referring to herself as an amateur photographer. Magazines want professional caliber pictures—usually color transparencies (slides). In this instance, if the magazine was sold on the article, it probably would arrange either to have pictures taken by a pro or, possibly, buy pictures from one of several companies that supply them to magazines and other customers.

HANDS ON

1. Write a query letter to a print consumer or trade magazine based on your article idea developed earlier.

2. Write an e-mail query to an online magazine based on the same idea or another.

3. Invite critique from fellow students working in small groups.

7 Writing to Be Read

You've done a powerful lot of writing in your scholastic and collegiate life: oodles of book reports, bunches of term papers, scads of essays, and perhaps a clip file full of college newspaper articles. But there is more to be learned about writing in general.

Maybe relearned.

The advice offered here is based on many years of reviewing the work of students at different writing stages: freshmen plodding through required courses in composition, research and argument; juniors and seniors tackling courses in their journalism or public relations major. It seems that some writing skills and habits are harder to acquire and practice than others. It is these devices you need to concentrate on now before you take on magazine article writing.

Active v. Passive Voice

The passive voice is frequently overused by many young writers. If you just exclaimed, "Gotcha!," you're right. That last sentence is written in the passive voice. It reads as follows in the active voice: Many young writers frequently overuse the passive voice.

The writer creates the passive voice when the main verb in the sentence denotes action performed on the subject. When the sentence is rewritten in the active voice, therefore, the subject performs the action. For example, study these three sets of sentences:

> *Set One*
> - The computer was turned on by him. (Passive)
> - He turned on the computer. (Active)
>
> *Set Two*
> - There was an article in the magazine on losing weight that she found particularly helpful. (Passive)
> - She found particularly helpful the magazine article on losing weight. (Active)

Set Three
- As it turned out, the fire labeled arson was started by a local fireman. (Passive)
- A local fireman started the fire labeled arson. (Active)

The last set of sentences in particular demonstrates how the active voice makes a sentence stronger, gets the reader directly to the point of the sentence. Now, examine these two sentences:

- There are countless patients who have been horribly butchered by careless, incompetent doctors.
- Careless, incompetent doctors have horribly butchered countless patients.

The first sentence, written in the passive voice, drains much of the force from the accusation. Also, note that two of the weakest sentences above begin with the phrase "there was" and "there are." Some purists absolutely forbid their students to begin a sentence with those phrases (and penalizes those who do). A rule of thumb, then: When you begin to write one of those phrases, stop and recast the sentence.

"Passive voice, also called passive construction, is an obstacle to clear writing for two reasons," writes Robin A. Cormier in her book *Error-Free Writing*: "It creates unnecessarily wordy sentences and it can dilute the impact of the writer's statement."

Passive construction, however, is occasionally desirable when your intention is to focus reader attention on the object of the action. For example:

- "Bleeding hearts" is what the senator called those who resented his vote.
- Drugs were found in her apartment by police.

In these two instances, the writer employed passive construction for emphasis, to call the reader's attention to what are, presumably, unexpected and startling revelations: Calling some persons bleeding hearts and the fact that drugs were discovered in the girl's apartment.

Verbs v. Adjectives

"The adjective hasn't been built that can pull a weak or inaccurate noun out of a tight place," wrote William Strunk Jr. and E. B. White in *The Elements of Style*. From our earliest writing, most of us have tended to rely on adjectives to describe what our senses acknowledge in our environment and to delight, excite, and titillate our readers. Very often we purposefully choose adjectives that we think are a cut or two above the ordinary: beauteous instead of merely pretty, clamorous instead of just loud.

Adjectives and adverbs are not to be shunned, but frequently a combination of noun and action verb are more satisfactory and more powerful in their impact upon the reader than a single adjective or adverb, even a string of them. Consider these examples:

Set One
- He was very muscular.
- His muscles bulged.

Set Two
- The mountain peaks were lofty.
- The mountain peaks stabbed the clouds.

Set Three
- The sunset was absolutely gorgeous.
- The setting sun dabbled the sky in soft pink and faded purple.

The second sentence in the third set employs adjectives effectively, but the verb energizes the description.

As is the case with any attempt to change habits, whether in writing or in any other aspect of our life, the movement has to be deliberate and thoughtful. If, then, you are to break your long-standing habit of leaning on adjectives and adverbs, you must stop in mid-sentence, or wherever the adjectives and adverbs occur, and consciously think of what combination of verb and noun or verb alone will work better.

Steer Clear of Cliches

In her book, Robin Cormier lists 300 cliches, from "ace in the hole" to "I wouldn't touch it with a 10-foot pole" (and "steer clear of"). Of course, a phrase becomes a cliche when people use it frequently, so you might purposefully use a cliche because you think your reader will have no trouble understanding your meaning. Wrong! Don't use the cliche; find a new and better way—your way—to express yourself. The writer who frequently uses cliches is an unimaginative and lazy writer.

Let's do something about the two cliches quoted above.

Original Sentence: "He wasn't afraid of the competition because his ace in the hole was a list of potential clients not available to the rival company."

The cliche could simply be left out of the sentence. Then it would read: "He wasn't afraid of the competition because he had a list of potential clients not available to the rival company." However, the writer of the original sentence might have used the cliche to convey the notion that the businessman in question was cagey and calculating. In that case, we might want to retain the implication as we rewrite the sentence to omit the cliche. One way to accomplish this would be to write the sentence as follows: "He wasn't afraid of the competition because only he had access to a list of potential clients."

Original Sentence: "Her friend expected her to react to his off-color remark, but she wouldn't touch it with a 10-foot pole."

Again, one way to rewrite the sentence is to leave out the cliche: "Her friend expected her to react to his off-color remark, but she didn't." However, the writer of the original sentence presumably included the cliche to show the person's extreme reluctance to react. Perhaps she did not want to give the man who uttered the off color remark the satisfaction of knowing he had accomplished his goal of shocking or embarrassing her. Or maybe she was afraid of what she might say in retort. In either case, the sentence could be rewritten to state the specific reason for her avoiding a response.

Avoid Syntax Sinkholes

Once in a while—well, fairly often for some persons—writers and their readers become mired in and totally confused by a sentence that seems endless and, ultimately, pointless. One reason it happens is because you aren't entirely sure where you are going with the sentence when you start it. You have a point to make, but you haven't thought it through very thoroughly or carefully. You have overlooked complications, asides, contradictions. Then, when you are unfortunately well into the sentence, these things suddenly occur to you. Rather than stopping and trying to figure out how best to handle your brainstorm, you stumble along trying to accommodate everything into the one sentence.

Clues that you are constructing monstrosities include two or more semicolons followed by "therefore," "however," "furthermore," or "in addition." Another clue is a preponderance of parenthetical clauses. Here is an example of a sentence dribbling into a bottomless sinkhole:

Many college students, especially those who have had minimal writing experience in high school, often have difficulty constructing sentences that express their views clearly and succinctly; their writing instructors regard correction of this problem to be their primary goal; however, the problem is exacerbated when other professors across campus, and this includes all disciplines, fail to attach as much importance to the structure of students' reports as they do to the substance, thereby reinforcing the idea some students have, not unexpectedly, that the two activities are separate, when of course they are inexorably connected.

Admittedly, this is a gross example, but it is not far-fetched. The main problem is that the writer's intention seems to change at mid-point—before the second semicolon. Until then, the writer explains the difficulty students have writing clear and succinct sentences. The conjunction "however" introduces the new, albeit related, point that writing skills are not considered very important by faculty in other disciplines who are more concerned about the content of reports on assigned topics. The long clause beginning "thereby reinforcing" injects a third point about the connection between what is written with how it is written.

If it is correct that the writer of the sentence initially intended simply to point out a problem with student writing, what happened was that these other points occurred to him as he was writing. Since they are related, he just kept plodding along, perhaps forgetting where he started and not knowing exactly where he was going to wind up. This particular sentence can be helped by breaking it apart into at least three separate sentences. An even better solution would be to devote perhaps a paragraph or more to each point so each could be properly developed through exposition and example.

Another reason readers get lost in a sentence is because the writer has separated the subject from the verb with qualifying and modifying clauses. Consider this horrendous example cited in the book *Ideas that Work* (McGraw-Hill Publications Company, 1972): "A final report on the results of last summer's preschool special education program, which was developed to assist both brain damaged children and those with limited mental retardation to attain maximum mental, physical and social growth, has been prepared."

The authors pointed out: "Placing the verb early in the sentence [helps] simplify sentence structure. Holding it to the end keeps the reader wondering about—and sometimes losing—the main point." They suggested beginning the sentence as follows: "A final report has been prepared on the results. . . ."

Strunk and White have the final say: "When you become hopelessly mired in a sentence, it is best to start fresh; do not try to fight your way through against the terrible odds of syntax. Usually, what is wrong is that the construction has become too involved at some point; the sentence needs to be broken apart and replaced by two or more shorter sentences."

Vague is Never in Vogue

Over the years, teachers have told students that the most damning criticism they can apply to their writing consists of just two words: "meaning unclear." The problem is that students sometimes leave out words, phrases, whole gobs of information that would elaborate, explain, and enlighten. The meaning is vague; the writing is confusing and the information is incomplete. Consider this paragraph:

The computer in the home poses many advantages and disadvantages. One way it might help is by giving parents more time with their children. Also, people can work at home, although that may take away from the office experience. One serious drawback is the prospect of people being by themselves most of the day. They might not have to go out of their home even to shop. What will happen when the computer monitor is also the television screen and every member of the family has a unit?

Readers' questions and missing answers might be as follows:

Q. Why will the computer give parents more time at home with their children, and so what?

A. Mothers and fathers working at home can be with their children instead of sending the little ones off to day care and allowing older ones to come home from school to an empty nest.

Q. What is the "office experience" that may be in danger?

A. Men and women working at home may lack the discipline usually present in the office, may be distracted by children and household chores, and may not be challenged and stimulated by other employees' ideas and suggestions.

Q. Why is being alone at home in front of the screen a problem?

A. Because humans are social animals. If boys and girls, men and women spend too much time alone, they may lose interpersonal skills necessary for home, office, and community to function effectively.

George Orwell, best known for his books *Animal Farm* and *Nineteen Eighty–four,* warned in an essay many years ago that writing was becoming increasingly abstract. Too many persons in public life, he said, had begun taking words that have specific meaning when standing alone or in certain contexts and stringing them together into sentences that come out as gibberish. The authors of *Ideas that Work* cited this sentence from a school district newsletter as a prime example of what Orwell was describing, "The implementation of a multi-faceted approach in the language arts program will effectuate an improvement in the communicative efforts of children."

Here are two tips for clarifying meaning in your writing:

Tip One: Substitute concrete terms for abstract ones.

• Instead of saying, as a student did in a query letter to a travel magazine, "I visited a myriad of significant places associated with some of the country's most important historical places," name the most significant places.

• Instead of saying, "A number of persons attended the fund-raising event, which netted more money than the sponsors had hoped for," state the figures.

Tip Two: Avoid jargon and technical terms unless you define them.

- The educator writing in the newsletter quoted used a term straight out of educationese (do they learn that language in college?)—"multi-faceted." He did not define what he meant.

- A student's query letter referred several times to the dangers of "performance enhancing drugs" without ever clearly stating what performance the drugs are intended to enhance, or how they are supposed to do it.

As with all writing, remember the reader. If you suspect your readers may not know the jargon or technical terms you are about to write, don't use them. Find another way to say the same thing.

FOR EXAMPLE

The opening paragraph of an article titled "A True Art Form" by student Nicole Cranston illustrates both active voice and use of verb and noun in description.

"It's midnight. The April wind whips through the tunnel that 'Comic' has crawled down into in order to escape the notice of anyone. He lands on the wet underground with a crash and stumbles to his feet. He picks the perfect spot and begins to work quickly until his masterpiece of colors and letters is complete. After he is finished, he must leave without a trace, for fear of being caught is constant in this way of life. This is the underground world of graffiti."

Student Kristen Finnie wrote several sentences in her article "The Hidden Jewel of the Crown" that effectively used nouns and verbs to describe.

Describing historic houses in Newcastle-Upon-Tyne: "Together they form a rich tapestry threading all the way up the steep northern cliffs of the river gorge."

Describing a venerable pub: "Once inside, you might be overpowered [by] the scent of 250 years worth of spilt alcohol and used up cigarettes. . . ."

Describing weekend crowds: "On Saturday and Sunday mornings people clutter the streets to buy and sell all sorts of different goods."

"Things You Can't Leave at Home," an article about the impact of American culture on Australian culture by student Ken McFarlane, also illustrates the use of verbs and nouns to describe.

"Much to my dismay, I would not be experiencing a good night out at a local pub cleansing my arteries with Victorian Bitter or Toohey's New. . . ."

"Imperialism is not dead; it just hides itself in a Gap jean, a Coke can, and a Lone Star food chain."

Here is how several professional writers wrote to be read:

From a profile titled "The Hell-Raiser" by John Cassidy in the September 11, 2000 issue of *The New Yorker*:

The New York *Post* columnist Steve Dunleavy keeps a desk just off the paper's newsroom, in an anonymous skyscraper on Sixth Avenue and Forty-seventh Street, but Langan's, an Irish bar just down the block, is his real office. In the five years that he has been going to Langan's, according to one employee, he has been spotted eating just once—a bowl of onion soup, ordered, quite possibly, in error. The ability to subsist on a diet largely restricted to alcohol and tobacco adds to the rakish image Dunleavy has cultivated during almost half a century in the news business, and so does his face, which is creased like an old pair of leather shoes. One evening earlier this summer, I walked into Langan's and picked him out at his favorite booth, a quiet one by the men's room. He was smartly dressed, in a gray three-piece suit, white monogrammed shirt with French cuffs, gold cufflinks, red silk tie, and shiny black shoes. His pallor was that of a rotting cod. His silver pompadour, which makes him resemble an aging Elvis impersonator, shot from his crown in glorious defiance of taste and gravity.

From an article titled "Send in the Clowns" by Leigh Buchanan in the September 2000 issue of *Inc.*:

Joe Keefe is a human dipstick: always testing his customers' comfort levels. Leaning back in his chair—his head almost brushing the casual tableau of bottles (aspirin, mouthwash, bourbon) arrayed on a shelf behind him—Keefe listens intently to Lauren Price, whose voice is being channeled through a speakerphone into his Chicago office. Price, director of sales development for *People* magazine, has retained Second City Communications (SCC) to run a workshop at her company's annual sales meeting, and she wants assurances from Keefe, the SCC cofounder, that no *People* employees will be made uncomfortable by, for example being required to fall backward into the arms of any other *People* employees or having to do anything alone on a stage. Solemnly, Keefe pledges that workshop participants will remain upright and in groups at all times. "We want your people to feel they're in a situation of total security," he tells Price, in the kind of soothing tones you'd expect to hear issuing through a confessional screen. "If you have any more questions, feel free to call back in the afternoon when we're sober."

Keefe's demeanor—pitched between the executive aplomb of King Lear and the irreverence of Lear's jester—is a business requirement given SCC's not-always-compatible audience and ancestry. SCC is the offspring of the Second City Inc., known for its edgy, improvization-driven shows. . . . SCC's audience is a different crowd—ordinarily straight-edged business folk engaged in the risky business of exposing their organizations' delicate sensibilities to the emotional and intellectual bungee jumping that is comedy.

H A N D S   O N

1. Examine any two consumer magazines (print or online) that contain features with particularly good description. Find examples where a combination of verbs and nouns has been used instead of or in conjunction with adjectives and adverbs.

   - Examine any two consumer or trade publications (print or online). Find examples where the writer has avoided what might have been long and confusing sentences by dividing a thought into two or more sentences.

   - Examine any two consumer or trade publications (print or online). Find examples where the writer has assisted the reader by defining terms or providing additional information that helps clarify meaning.

2. Go over some of your recent descriptive writing. Where you have relied primarily on adjectives and adverbs, try enhancing and invigorating the description by rewriting the passages using verbs and nouns.

   - Go over some of your recent writing and keep an eye out for cliches. If you find any, come up with a new way to say the same thing.

   - Go over some of your recent writing and find examples of extra long sentences. Divide those whoppers into two or more sentences and see if that doesn't improve readability and understanding.

   - Go over some of your recent writing and find instances where your reader(s) might have been better served if you had defined terms or provided additional information.

CHAPTER

8 Writing the Article

William Strunk Jr. and E. B. White had it about right when, in their classic guide to good writing *The Elements of Style,* they stated, "The approach to style is by way of plainness, simplicity, orderliness, sincerity." Now, tack on this addendum: The approach to magazine writing style is by way of whatever is dictated by the editors of the magazines for which you're writing.

For example, this is how the editors of two men's magazines described their publication's style for their listing in *Writer's Market 2000:*

Heartland USA: "relaxed, jocular, easy-to-read."

Maxim: "irreverence, edge and humor."

Every editor, without exception, urges persons who wish to write for their publication to read one or more issues to get a sense not only of the kinds of articles they favor, but the writing style they prefer. The more you read a magazine the more likely its writing style will rub off on you—infuse your writing. Hear Strunk and White again: "Never imitate consciously, but do not worry about being an imitator; take pains instead to admire what is good. Then when you write in a way that comes naturally, you will echo the halloos [expressions] that bear repeating."

Several years ago at a workshop for editors and staff writers employed by a group of magazines, the leader offered Strunk and White's advice concerning imitation. Someone asked the leader who he unconsciously imitated. He answered that his role models would not—probably could not—also be theirs. You have to shape your writing according to the styles you admire or aspire to. If your goal is to write the kinds of how-to articles that are the guts of many magazines, then read the best of that kind of writing and you will likely find yourself slipping more easily into that groove. On the other hand, if you want to try your hand at writing for some of the leading trade publications, select a few in those fields of your special interest and begin reading them regularly. Perhaps your aim is to write for those magazines that contain long articles laden with the fruits of tireless research and that are written in a style that approaches the best non-fiction. Read their authors.

One of the words Strunk and White did not include in their definition of style is creativity, but that word and similar expressions cropped up often when a group of magazine editors was asked to tell how writing feature articles for magazines differs from writing news articles for newspapers. The editors were asked about the difference because many students of magazine article writing also have taken or are taking courses in news reporting or something similar.

Here are what some editors had to say concerning the difference between writing magazine features and hard news:

- "More room for personal voice and creativity in magazine [writing]."
  —Susan Costars, managing editor, *Specialty Travel Index*
- "Magazine article writing takes more imagination."
  —Roberta Redford, editor, *Contemporary Songwriter Magazine*
- "More possibility for creative approaches [in magazine feature writing]."
  —Jon C. Hatter, editor, *Scouting Magazine*
- "Newspaper writing tends to be more sterile than magazine writing. Tighter space in newspapers isn't conducive to the creativity offered by magazines."
  —Wesley S. Abravanel, managing editor, *Porthole Cruise Magazine*

Imitate Good Writing

Many years ago I was among a group of recent college graduates fresh from journalism courses and stints as editors of our college newspapers who became cub reporters on *The Record*, New Jersey's second largest newspaper. We thought we were pretty good—very good, in fact. Then we began to read the daily column by William A. Caldwell, whose body of work eventually earned him a Pulitzer Prize. Caldwell's style was plain, simple, and orderly all right—and always sincere, but what set his writing apart was the way he crafted a sentence, how he demonstrated that writing, while being plain and simple, also can be creative. But he did not create by stretching for and stringing together fancy words; he never casually plucked words with obscure meanings from long lists in *Roget's Thesaurus,* nor did he try to impress his readers by affecting the style of fiction writers. He created memorable sentences by using ordinary words in an extraordinary way—phrases and sentences of his own, unique invention.

In 1971, for example, newspaper editorials across the country castigated the Nixon Administration for its attempt to prevent the *New York Times* and *Washington Post* from publishing the so-called Pentagon Papers that were highly critical of the government's role in the Vietnam War. Caldwell, in his column, lamented that he could not recognize an American government that would seek to prevent the press from exercising its freedom guaranteed by the Constitution. His column was titled "Who Let This Bum into the House?" and it commenced as follows: "It's embarrassing, and I suppose the lapse is attributable to my bad habit of having birthdays so often, but doggoned if I would ever have recognized this barrelchested, bullet-headed, bemedaled goon that's lumbering around introducing himself as my government." Plain, simple, and creative.

In addition to unconsciously imitating good writing, here are other steps you can take to help you write a more polished, professional magazine article.

Rely More on a Personal, Conversational Voice and Tone

Magazine writing allows for more intimacy between writer and reader. This is true not only for how-to and personal experience/opinion pieces, but for nearly all writing in consumer publications and even in trade and professional publications. Robin A. Cormier's book *Error-Free Writing* is addressed primarily to writers for trade publications. In it, she states: "Write as if you are having a face-to-face conversation with your readers."

That is not to suggest the kind of disjointed, often slangy conversation one might carry on in a dorm room or over beers at the local watering hole. Instead, what is meant is conversation in which the speaker/writer is conscious of using language correctly and cares that the listener/reader fully understands every word and experiences every emotion. In his textbook *Writing for Magazines,* (Prentice-Hall, 1993), now out of print, Myrick E. Land recounts how the author Tom Wolfe wrote one of his very first articles, a piece about custom-built cars for *Esquire* magazine in 1963: "When Wolfe seemed unable to make a start on the article, Byron Dobell, an experienced and sympathetic editor, offered a suggestion. Wolfe could just type up his notes, telling Dobell what he had seen and heard and observed [while researching for the article in New York and California], and drop these pages off at the *Esquire* offices." Wolfe accepted the suggestion and wrote the memo—like almost any memo—as though he were talking directly to Dobell. Although the memo was "unorthodox and somewhat shapeless," Dobell basically dropped the "Dear Byron" at the start of the 20-page memo and published it almost verbatim under the equally unorthodox title "There Goes (Vrooom! Vroom!) That KandyKolored (Thphhhhhh!) Tangerine-Flake Streamline Baby (Rahghhh!) Around the Bend (Brummmmmmmmmm-mmmmmmmmm) . . . "

At one point in their valuable, skinny book, Strunk and White refer to style as "the sound words make on paper." Just as the conversationalist expects her spoken words to impact the listener even as they swirl past his ears, so the writer seeks to have her words ring off the printed page. Strunk and White offer a little exercise in which they try to rewrite Thomas Paine's memorable line during the American Revolution: "These are the times that try men's souls." Their four attempts, by their own admission, fall short. However, they puzzle over why the rewrites don't read as well (or sound as good).

"No fault of grammar can be detected in them, and in every case the meaning is clear. Each version is correct, and each, for some reason that we can't readily put our finger on, is marked for oblivion." They conclude that the reasons why some words, phrases, and sentences sing and others simply drone may forever remain a mystery.

Rely More on Direct Quotation

If you have come to magazine article writing from other journalism classes, you should have a greater appreciation for direct quotation. However, if you have somehow leapfrogged over news writing or news reporting, you may be suffering from what might be called "comp-lag." This is a condition whereby the student, like the traveler who has just flown between widely separated time zones, finds himself slightly disoriented. After spending years writing compositions and term papers where the ideas and views of others originate in print sources and are primarily summarized and paraphrased, he finds it difficult to adjust to a writing style that demands quoting live sources verbatim.

A major part of the problem, of course, is that students of magazine article writing who have not experienced news reporting are generally frightened at the prospect of interviewing someone. The interview can be intimidating for even the experienced journalist, particularly when the interviewer has only the most superficial knowledge of the subject about which he is asking the questions. Nevertheless, most magazine articles rely on direct quotation of persons who are in some way integral to telling the story.

A female student who also worked as a cheerleader for a major professional team wrote an article about one of the few male cheerleaders on the squad whose primary role is to lift and throw the women during strenuous routines. The angle was that fans rarely see and appreciate the male cheerleaders, especially if they watch a game on television. The camera's eye is almost always focused on the skimpy outfits worn by the women. The problem with the student's article draft was that she told about the male cheerleader's function, explained how he felt about being overlooked and unseen, and described how women react to a male colleague. After reviewing the draft, the student's instructor told her to rewrite the article by telling the male cheerleader's story in his own words. She had to let him and his female co-workers talk!

"Weak articles often make little or no use of direct quotes," stated Myrick Land in his textbook *Writing for Magazines*. "Quotes must be used selectively, and there is no point in including those that are dull, rambling, or confusing. But, in general, writers should realize that they are losing a valuable element in an article if they fail to make some use of direct quotes."

Perhaps you've read—or written—sports articles that tell what is happening and describe what it's like to be a part of the happening. It can sometimes get downright boring, because the writer on the sidelines, no matter how enthusiastic or capable, cannot generate the feelings that are better expressed by the participants. On the other hand, see—and hear—what it's like when the writer stops talking and allows the people in his story to speak.

Jerry Gibbs is a staff writer for *Outdoor Life.* For his article "Go Ahead, Make My Day" in the April 1999 issue, Gibbs went along when Captain Jake Jordon took fisherman Lee Leone out to sea to catch tarpon. Gibbs could merely have described what it's like to go after tarpon, but, instead, he let Jordon do most of the talking, not just because he was the expert, but because Jordon's words added salt to the story. Remember how Strunk and White talked about the sound words make on paper? Listen.

"The job of the tarpon," says Jake, "is to show just enough of themselves to completely unnerve you . . . like those over there giving me the fin. Look at them. 'Here's for you, Captain Jake.' Eleven o'clock, cast. Never mind, too late. My job is to get you to the point where even though you're going crazy inside, you can perform."

And later when they spot a pod of fish. "There's a tarpon. He shook his fin—'Ha ha, Captain Jake, you can't see me.' " The fish get closer. "Happy pigs. Rolling. Heads up. Still giving me the fin."

Lest you think direct quotation is only, or mostly, for consumer magazines, be advised that articles in trade publications can also benefit. Doug Newsom and Tom Siegfried were talking to people who write for both trade and consumer publications in their book *Writing in Public Relations Practice: Form & Style* (Wadsworth Publishing Company, 1981): "Another way to break monotony and make writing more natural is to use direct quotations. Quotations help make the writing more personal, more like conversation, and therefore more readable."

While magazine articles generally read better when persons interviewed are quoted directly, be careful not to overdo quotation. Here are a few guidelines on when to quote a source:

- When you cannot possibly improve upon what the source said.
- When the source's statement adds color and sparkle to the article.
- When the source says something so outrageous or offbeat that if you were to paraphrase it, your readers would think you misquoted the source. For example, suppose Michael Jordan, in his heyday, said in an unguarded moment, "I wear several different kinds of sneakers, not just Nike."

When you have two or more sentences of direct quotation in a row, identify the speaker (source) at the beginning or end of the first sentence. Do not wait until the end of the second, third or fourth sentence to tell your reader who is being quoted. Readers don't appreciate being kept in the dark.

Combining Direct Quotation and Narration

Newsom and Siegfried also suggested, "Often it is best to make a point in your own words and then use a quotation to amplify or illustrate." Their point, which is similar to Myrick Land's, is not to overuse direct quotation, especially if it does not add reality and zest to the writing. Teachers of composition often advise their students not to quote print sources verbatim when they can report the information just as well in their own paraphrase or summary.

Returning to Jerry Gibbs' article about fishing for tarpon, the following excerpt demonstrates how a good writer combines direct quotation and narration. Captain Jake is telling fisherman Leone to ignore the pod of fish Leone has spotted:

"Not worth chasing them. There'll be more coming." And there are. The mullet migration is over. The tarpon have shifted from north-south up and down the Keys, to east-west near the bridges where Jakes teaches. With the easy pickings of mullet gone, the big fish are on the flats more, circling in daisy chains, instincts sliding toward sex. They are more vulnerable to fly. The Captain is happy. "I try to stay with the big, happy schools, poling, using the electrics, but in this area you first try to ambush them. It's like elk hunting— with a bow." And so we go on stand . . . we anchor.

Another example of when and how to merge narration and direct quotation comes from the article "For The Early Show, It's Getting Late" by Gay Jervey in the May 2000 issue of *Brill's Content*. The article describes how Bryant Gumbel, host of the "The Early Show" on CBS in the morning, does not relate well with many of the show's staff members while at the same time antagonizing many viewers:

As cordial and charming as Gumbel can be when he so desires, these days he is known among the staff of the struggling "The Early Show" for an echoing inaccessibility, to the point that all but his fellow on-air talent and top producers correspond with him largely through e-mail, and, even then, only when necessary.

"The unwritten rule was you could e-mail Gumbel but were to have no direct contact," remembers a former "Early Show" producer. "You were not to call him."

"Bryant can be the most jovial guy on e-mail, but you can't talk to him." says a current employee of The Early Show. "He just does not deal with anybody."

What Jervey has done, and what other writers of magazine articles do regularly, is pretty much what Newsom and Siegfried suggested: Use the verbatim quotation to illustrate and amplify a point made by the author. Another way to state this is that direct quotation from persons interviewed by the writer attest to the truthfulness or accuracy of the writer's own observations and conclusions. In the case of Jervey's article, for example, the entire piece argues that Gumbel's aloofness, which no one can quite explain, is the primary cause of the show's lack of appeal. The statements by the former and present staffer are evidence that supports that conclusion.

Rely More on Anecdotes

A cursory reading of consumer magazines and even many trade publications reveals how much they rely on anecdotes to illustrate points made by the author. In fact, we could begin this section with an anecdote—a very brief account of an incident—taken from the classroom:

As he pored over his article draft, Joe sensed something was missing, but he couldn't put his finger on it. He had solid information and good quotes from a couple of sources, but they weren't enough somehow. He asked Liz, who sat next to him in class, to read the draft and see if she could spot the trouble. It didn't take her long: "You talk about the problem and you have lots of statistics, but what you don't have and need is an example of how someone gets himself into that kind of mess in the first place." Joe followed Liz's suggestion, and it worked. He could tell that the anecdote about a friend's dilemma would help his readers better understand and appreciate the dimensions of the problem.

Don't confuse an anecdote with a narrative. Some articles include long narratives that tell a story that involves either the author or someone else. The narrative also is illustrative of the point(s) the author is making, but it may go on for a number of paragraphs. The typical anecdote, however, is not much longer than the one about Joe. And the anecdote is about a single incident, whereas the narrative might involve more than one event; indeed, it might tell a story that spans weeks, months, or years.

The anecdote can be humorous or deadly serious, or somewhere in between. What it accomplishes in a way that no other writing device can do quite so effectively is to show the reader how one person or a group of persons was actually affected by or affected the subject the author is writing about. Consider this anecdote that begins a student's query letter suggesting an article about organ and tissue donation:

It was a brisk but sunny January day when Melissa and a few of her friends completed their mid-term exams. Normally, juniors were not allowed to drive to school, but during exam week they were, so they could leave right after their exams. The girls left school early and decided to go out for breakfast to celebrate, but they never made it there. Before they reached the diner, the girls got into a terrible accident. Melissa, only 16, was just beginning her life [when] she was tragically killed. Her spirit lives on now not only in the memories of friends and family, but also in people she never met, people whose lives she saved. You see, Melissa was an organ and tissue donor."

The *Journal of Telecommunications in Higher Education* is a publication of the Association for Telecommunications Professionals in Higher Education. Its Spring 2000 issue included an article on how the Americans with Disabilities Act "mandates handling of communications resources for the disabled." The article is mostly straightforward reporting, but the author, Curt Harler, early on made the reader realize what compliance with the law really means in terms of its impact on real people's lives. He did it with this anecdote:

A coed [at Southwestern University in the mid-1960s], out on a date, was in danger of missing curfew and finding herself in a lot of trouble. At the edge of campus is a railroad track, and, in a hurry, she and her date raced a locomotive and lost. She broke both legs, an arm, some ribs, and her jaw, and suffered head injuries and lost teeth. When she finally returned to school, she was in a wheelchair. Although wheelchair access was not then mandated by law, at least two buildings—the administration building in which many classes were held and the dorm—were outfitted with ramps just for her.

Newsom and Siegfried in their book aimed at public relations practitioners offer this advice: "One of the best devices for involving the reader in a piece of writing is the anecdote. As Stanford professor Bill Rivers says, "No other element of an article is more important." Anecdotes break monotony, illustrate points, and give the reader something to visualize. If they deal with familiar things, anecdotes can help people relate to the subject of the article. Anecdotes "show" readers something rather than merely tell about it.

Case Studies Are Also Helpful

A case study is similar to an anecdote in that it illustrates a point by recounting what happened to one or more individuals. However, it differs from an anecdote in at least two ways: (1) it may not be confined to a single incident, and (2) it often reflects extensive research. In psychology and sociology, for example, case studies may be clinical, probing causes for human behavior.

Bruce Ballenger, author of *The Curious Researcher* (Allyn & Bacon, 1994), points out that research results are "often peopleless landscapes, which is one of the things that can make them so lifeless to read." He suggests case studies as a means of resuscitating moribund research. "Ultimately, what makes almost any topic matter to the writer or the reader is what difference it makes to people."

The November 1998 issue of *The Rotarian* published an article by Cary Silver that described the outstanding work of Dr. Catherine Hamlin at a private hospital in Ethiopia. Dr. Hamlin's skills are devoted almost exclusively to helping young women who suffer from fistula, a complication of childbirth. The case study of one woman takes up most of the two-page article. It describes how fistula occurred, how the condition affected the woman's life, and how, after surgery, she was able to exclaim: "When I first heard that I could have children again, I cried tears of joy."

Rely More on Development

The group of editors surveyed, when describing the difference between writing news articles for a newspaper and writing features for magazines, pointed out that the magazine article writer is able to be more creative. They might have added that magazine articles also allow and encourage the writer to more fully develop all aspects of the story. These include characters and scenes. Much like the fiction writer.

Characters.   Except in the case of a special feature or profile, the newspaper staff writer working on a news article usually talks to people for the purpose of gathering information about the subject of the article. What, when, where, why, and how questions, therefore, are critical. Who questions may be important only insofar as identifying the people as credible sources. Also, the news writer frequently is constrained by space. There simply isn't room for many details about how people look and act. On the other hand, people are more than sources of information for the magazine article writer. They are integral to the story. Who becomes as important as the other four w's, sometimes more so. Therefore, the writer pays close attention not only to what people say, but also to their appearance and demeanor. Just as the fiction writer wants readers to "see" characters—get inside them—so does the magazine article writer. Plus, the magazine usually affords the writer more space for detailed descriptions.

Consider this scenario: The year is 1999, and a news writer and a magazine writer have both scheduled an appointment (on different days) at the offices of the Nederlander Organization on West 53rd Street in New York City. Both want to talk to James Nederlander, Sr. and his son about their multi-million-dollar company that owns and operates more legitimate theaters in America than anyone else. The news writer knows she can count on a maximum 15 column inches for her story, or approximately 900 words, and so she will have to limit her focus pretty much to the business itself—questions about when the Nederlanders founded the organization, how they built it up, and what its current status is. On the other hand, the magazine writer is working on a major feature that may jump to several pages. His story is going to be as much about the Nederlanders as about their business. He has both the intent and the space, therefore, to develop character.

Eric Konigsberg, contributing editor at *New York* magazine, wrote just such a story for the May 31, 1999 issue, and here is how he described Jimmy

Nederlander, the founder: "Jimmy is an owlish 77 years old, and these days is somewhat frail, the result of a stroke he suffered ten years ago. He is short, about five foot five or six, with the adenoids to match; wears square-shaped, clear plastic eyeglasses; and walks with an aluminum cane, slowly, bringing one step even with the other before moving forward."

Myrick Land, in his out-of-print book *Writing for Magazines,* reflects on how "traditional journalists"—including most newspaper writers—"limit their descriptions of people in their articles to a few factual details (age, height, hair color, occupation, and so forth). On the other hand, so-called 'new journalists'—including most magazine writers—often include many additional details about dress, personal appearance, behavior and possessions."

Scenes.   Unlike the news writer, the magazine writer also records scenes in detail, for example an office layout (furniture, wall hangings, objects on a desk top). Again, it is important to the magazine writer that his readers are able to "see" where characters work or play, where the action takes place. "Akin to telling a story is a description that arouses curiosity," writes Richard Marius in his book *A Writer's Companion* (McGraw-Hill, 1999). "The reader wants to know, 'What exactly is happening here?' 'Why is this significant?' The scene must be interesting in itself."

Therefore, while the magazine writer is recording what people are telling him, he also is taking note of significant features in the surroundings. Significant insofar as they say something about the people. Consider this excerpt from the article "The Most Hated Lawyer" by Alan Deutschman that appeared in the February 1997 edition of *GQ:* The writer is interviewing lawyer Bill Lerach in his office:

So here we are, in Lerach's office at Milberg Weiss Bershad Hynes & Lerach, and there's paper everywhere. Red file dockets cover the floor and the rolling library carts and even the ledges along the crescent-shaped sweep of windows overlooking the San Diego waterfront. Ominously, each docket is marked with the name of a business that may soon get Lerached.

The scene pictured says something about the way the man works—hard, long hours—and the nature of his work—meticulous research.

FOR EXAMPLE

For the second major assignment in his magazine article writing class, junior Bryan Littel interviewed his friend, a rehabilitated drug user, over a period of days. The extended interview was taped. His article expertly blends narration and direct quotation. He queried five magazines, including *Rolling Stone, Reader's Digest,* and *College Bound.*

"Portrait of a User"
by Bryan Littel
(reprinted by permission of the author)

James (not his real name) remembers very clearly the first time he used cocaine. "It was like inhaling a freight train through your nose," he said. "After that, I felt very good, a sort of all-over tingling that makes you extremely happy. You could get hit by a truck when you're in that state and not really notice it."

Reality set in a few hours later when he came down from the high. "The word 'crash' gets thrown around a lot," he said in describing what it feels like. "That doesn't do it justice. Imagine parachuting out of a plane, except you're not wearing a chute and you're dropping 15,000 feet to Fifth Avenue in New York. And then, after you hit the ground, you bounce a few times."

This began the worst times in James's life: the darkening spiral of addiction and addict behavior. Up to that point, he had been a minor drug user, occasionally smoking marijuana and drinking. "Much like every other college student," he said.

James began his freshman year of college as a very promising student. He was an Eagle Scout, had played trumpet very successfully throughout high school, and, despite his attention deficit disorder, was one of a select few freshmen in his school's biotechnology program. "I wanted to be a biochemist," he said. "I wanted to cure the cancer I saw kill my grandfather and so many others."

Not too far into the semester, James got involved in a fraternity on campus and started drinking on a regular basis, which he said was no big deal. "I wasn't pledging, so I wasn't subject to the night-after-night schedule of drinking." Still, the nights of partying at the frat house eventually led to his first experience with drugs.

One evening at the house, with several of his friends from his dorm, someone brought out a few joints and passed them out. James took one, interested to see what it would do. "Simple experimentation," he said. "I won't say that marijuana was the 'gateway drug' that so-called experts label it, but it opened me to experimentation."

Marijuana had a very calming, mellowing effect on James. "In a lot of ways, it was a good thing for me," he said. "It kept me from bouncing off the walls, and I could actually keep my mind on one thing at a time. Unfortunately, the one thing was usually the texture of my bedroom ceiling and not my chem lab."

James remained active in other ways, even while ignoring his classes. He acted in several plays, played in the school's pep band, and played racquetball with his roommate on a regular basis. "Basically, I was concentrating on the things I was motivated to do," he said. "I don't know what effect the drinking and pot had on my motivation, but I had no problem going to rehearsals and getting to the student gym."

At the end of his first semester of college, James managed to fail all his classes except for biology, in which he got a B-plus. The drinking and marijuana had a lot to do with those failing grades, he acknowledges. "They weren't the only cause, though. The simple fact that I didn't bother going to class probably did me in more than anything."

Left with a minuscule GPA and the strong possibility of getting kicked out of college, James and his parents sought help. James's advisor and the dean of students met with them, and a tentative agreement was reached. James could stay in school for the next semester, but couldn't participate in any school-sanctioned activities. "That was an absolute joke," he said. "It was like they were saying. 'Here, don't do anything useful with your time. Go get wrecked and smoke up more often.' Not that any of them knew about my drinking or smoking, but the decision made no sense."

Somehow, though, James made it through the next semester without failing all his classes. "I surprised myself," he said. Even with the same drug and drinking habits from the previous semester, he passed four out of the five classes he took, and the school allowed him back for the next fall.

It was late September that James took his big step to cocaine, something that came about because of his roommate, Steve. "Steve lived down the hall from me the year before that, and he was my primary source of marijuana," James said. "Living with him in the fall, though, I found out he was connected to every kind of drug that anyone used on campus. He dealt, he used, you name it."

All during this time, James's family and friends had very little clue what was going on. His friends knew he was drinking, but dismissed that as nothing. His friend Mark said, "A college student who drinks a bit and parties at a frat house regularly isn't anything out of the ordinary." Some of them suspected something more was going on but couldn't say for sure. As his friend Alan put it, "You could tell there was something affecting James and changing him slowly and subtly."

Those slow, subtle changes soon became hideously obvious to everyone. James had a near repeat of his first semester of college, except this time he failed every class. "And quite miserably," he added. He was kicked out of school and reality came crashing down.

About a month after getting kicked out of school, James was pulled over for a speeding violation. "The cop spotted a few dime bags on top of my arm rest. They hadn't held any drugs, but I was charged with possession of drug paraphernalia." James's court date came two weeks later. The judge ordered him to go into pretrial intervention to clean his record and prevent him from further violations. "It wasn't a bad idea," James said. "In fact, it was a fairly good idea. It just wasn't a workable idea to an addict, which is what I had become."

James stopped using drugs for a short while because of the pretrial intervention program, but couldn't quit entirely. His parents had learned to figure out when he was using and when he wasn't and gave him random drug tests. "We weren't happy about having to do that," said his mother, "but really, we had tried to support James during his college troubles and even further, and that didn't work. We had to do something."

They soon realized he was still using, but there was little they could do about it. James was pulled over again for speeding, and police again noticed paraphernalia in his car. He claimed it was old stuff that hadn't been used, a story he repeated to his parents, his friends, and, later, to a judge.

"Yes, it was a complete lie," he admitted, "but it's what I believed in my head. As bizarre as it sounds, when you're an addict, you really believe all the garbage you spit at other people."

He went to court for this violation and was ordered into a rehab program. "It made sense, and it was the right decision." He started attending rehab sessions and got a job as a clerk in an Eckerd store. Court hassles continued to dog him, though. "You never hear about the minor details, you know, like a $1,300 fee for rehab and the fact that they want to take away your license. It's paradoxical."

Fortunately for James, the court decided to wait on suspending his license until after his rehab program was over the following October. He remained angry about what the court didn't tell him. "You think these people want to help addicts get clean, and then they throw this crap at you. I got lucky and they decided to be lenient, but what about the poor guy that doesn't get the court's mercy and has to make it to work and rehab without a car? It's ridiculous."

Rehab itself differed from what he expected. "I pictured either some neo-hippie commune thing or a prison camp atmosphere. Instead, it was more like a school, only you weren't learning math and writing, you were learning how to get off drugs."

It was also more difficult than James expected. His getting clean wasn't incredibly difficult, but seeing others like himself and worse was extremely wearing on him. "Seeing those people day in and day out, how pathetic they were; it was almost impossible," he said. "The heroin addicts were the worst. We lost at least seven in the months I was there. Very few manage to kick it for good."

He also saw the darker side of rehab—the addicts that came in and still managed to use the entire time they were going through the process. "It really wasn't that hard to trick their system into thinking you were clean. Drug tests were random, but took a week to come back, so you had a week to binge." He went on to say that if you had a young counselor, you had a better chance of getting away with using your drug of choice. "Even the trained, experienced counselors don't spot every instance of someone using."

Still, the combination of those counselors and the other addicts helped James in his recovery. "You really get a sense of how pathetic you've become when you're staring at someone just like you," he said. He went on to explain that sessions of rehab are somewhat like the "group therapy" images in television and movies, but they're far more intense than anything that's shown on-screen. "People will regularly scream at themselves and others during sessions," he said. "It doesn't usually turn into much more than people yelling 'mother-fucker' at each other."

One individual sticks out in his mind as being influential in the process—a fellow addict, a heroin user named Justin. "He was younger than me, which was scary. When he came in the first time, I thought I was looking at a reanimated corpse." They worked through the process together, with James helping Justin out as much as possible.

"I hated what I did to myself after I saw what happened to Justin," James said. That became a key factor in James's steps back from the world of drugs. Walking Justin through those first steps of rehab "was probably the most important, worthwhile action I'd taken in a year or more," said James. When he left rehab four months later, James made sure to keep in contact with Justin, who turned out to be one of the few heroin addicts who managed to kick the drug for good. "I'm proud of that," James said. "Even if drugs caused me to do a lot of bad, they gave me a chance to reclaim some good."

Now that he's clean, James is trying to move forward with his life. His plans are to go to medical school and become an ER doctor in the hopes that he'll be able to save lives, much like his was saved. "Drugs wrecked too many years of my life. I can't go back. I'll always be an addict, but I'll never go back."

Another college junior, Susan N. Carter, who is a pilot herself, wrote an article about fighting forest fires from small airplanes. The article, which features her pilot father, was intended for an aviation trade magazine. Carter also nicely blends direct quotation and narration.

"Charlie 2–Drop!"
by Susan N. Carter
(reprinted by permission of the author)
"Charlie 2–drop!" After flying over the high flames and through the ash and smoke, Ed Carter, Sr. flew back to the airstrip to refill the plane with fire retardant and returned to the forest fire to fight the flames again. "We are the other fire bombers," said Carter. "Most people know about the large airplanes in the west fighting forest fires, but how many know about the small, single engine tankers which fight forest fires in other areas?"

New Jersey is one such area, where a fleet of ten single engine tankers, two helicopter tankers, and three helicopter observation-command post crafts are operated. During fire season, which runs from March to May, some of these aircraft have been known to make up to fifty loads a day.

Ag planes began being used for the New Jersey Forest Fire Service in 1961. Since there were many fires in remote areas, something was needed for rapid, initial attack. "We decided to use aircraft so that we could get in and make a drop as soon as possible," said State Forest Fire Warden David Harrison. "Also, when people started building in the Pinelands and they started getting developments, we had to change the way we fight fire."

Ag planes are great for rapid initial attack because they can get in under the smoke. "A combination of planes and good pilots do really, really good. They do what we want them to do," said Harrison. "Airplanes do the job if there are good pilots to fly them, and having a fire fighting background doesn't hurt either. It shows if you have a firefighter first and a pilot second, because they know what area of the fire needs to be attacked first. They know what the fire is doing by the color of the smoke, they know when our guys are on the ground, and where to drop to help them out." Fire fighting background for a pilot is a definite plus.

As helpful as these ag planes have been, and are, at one time during the late 1960s to early '70s, the New Jersey Forest Fire Service did away with ag planes and relied on helicopters. The reason for this was because airplanes have to go back to a field in order to reload, whereas helicopters can reload their drop bucket at the nearest water supply. But ag planes reemerged because the helicopters were too expensive. Today, three ag planes can be run for the same cost as one chopper.

New Jersey is one of only a few states that actually has a forest fire program. Some of the other states include Florida, North and South Carolina, and California. The states without this service rely only on volunteer ground firefighters to fight their fires. Many of New Jersey's forest fire pilots have been sent out of state to fight out-of-control forest fires. Pilots Mike Dix, Charles Zielke, and Ed Carter, Jr. were some of those pilots sent to Long Island, New York, for thirteen days in 1995 to control fires in The Hamptons. "The residents of the towns surrounding the fire treated us all like heroes. They greeted us with cheers when we got out of our airplanes. With that, I knew we had done our job," pilot Ed Carter, Jr. remembered proudly.

"We're known nationally by the fire fighting world as being the top firefighters because of the way we fight fires," said Harrison. "Our expertise is recognized nationally and our individuals are recognized by name."

Fire has to be fought aggressively. A good ground crew and good pilots make a great fire fighting team. The ten Grumman Ag-Cat airplanes used by the Forest Fire Service are supplied by Downstown Airport in Vineland, New Jersey. These planes are maintained by a team of four mechanics in order to ensure safety and availability. Downstown Airport hosts the annual forest fire meeting for pilots and district fire wardens. This meeting is a way for pilots and ground crews to discuss drop technique, chemicals, and safety, with safety being paramount. Safety is stressed for both pilots and ground crews. No matter how big the blaze, it cannot be controlled without a safe operation.

When a ground crew receives a fire call from one of the fire towers, a section forest fire warden will often have a plane dispatched to the scene. This can be considered a safety precaution because the pilot will arrive on the scene before the ground crew and view the area from above first. Section Forest Fire Warden C-9, Bill Donnelly stated, "We depend highly on the pilots to be our eyes in the sky. They help us with our initial assessment as to what the fire is doing and where it's going. We depend on them greatly to get us out of a bind if we find ourselves in a situation that we shouldn't be in. We depend on them to come bail us out by putting the fire out around the trucks." Again, this is why good pilots and good ground crews make great fire fighting teams.

"Our job is not just fire suppression," explained forest fire pilot Charlie 1, Mike Dix. "I think it's equally important and advantageous to the Forest Fire Service that we can be on the scene in such a hurry. We're quite often the first ones there and that makes all the difference in the world. Many times these guys on the ground don't know what they're getting into; they just know that there's smoke and they have to go find it in the woods somewhere. And just by virtue of us being able to lead them to it, or explain what it looks like, that's a big benefit."

A tanker pilot carries an important job, no doubt, and that can be overlooked sometimes. It is not an easy job, and it is certainly not without danger. "Being a tanker pilot is hours of boredom interspersed with seconds of sheer terror," explained Ed Carter, Sr., Charlie 2, a tanker pilot with the Forest Fire Service for 25 years. "Days may go by without a single fire call, but you have to be standing by . . . waiting. But when a call comes in, I run for the plane, start the engine, check the tank to be sure it's full, take off, and head for the fire."

A major forest fire with so much heat can generate its own wind and make the flying hazardous. Carter added, "Winds generated by forest fires have been clocked at up to eighty miles an hour. This, along with thermals rising from the fire, keeps a pilot's hands full." Fighting fires from the sky is a serious danger. A pilot has to be ready for any situation. No two fires are alike.

Above all things, a forest fire pilot has to have experience. Of course, the only way to gain experience is to get out on a fire and try. Pilots are going to sometimes miss making a drop directly on the fire. Pilots have to be prepared to be criticized by the ground crews and by fellow pilots. But how else is a pilot going to learn? As State Forest Fire Warden Dave Harrison says, "My motto is, 'Good judgment is based on experience, and most experience is based on bad judgment.' I have that sign hanging on my office door." That is a great motto because it is true, and that is how pilots and ground crews alike learn.

"Charlie 2–drop! Heading back to base."

"Received Charlie 2, come on home."

At the end of a long day, Ed Carter, Sr. returns to the airport knowing that he has a job that saves precious land, trees, homes, animals, and lives.

A good example of a writer paying attention to character and scene is the article "I Was a Biker Babe Once." It was written by Desiree Dunne, a college junior at the time. Also, notice the personal, conversational style.

"I Was a Biker Babe Once"
by Desiree Dunne
(reprinted by permission of the author)
Freedom! In a word, that sums it up. The first time I straddled the leather seat and felt it vibrate between my legs as the wind whipped my hair into a wild mass of knots, I felt free. It's a glorious feeling. A feeling unlike any other. Those that haven't felt rain drops pelt their face like razors or felt their skin flap in the wind like a bowl of Jello, cannot possibly imagine what it feels like to really ride a motorcycle.

I'm a different person now. I used to be one of those people that contributed to the prejudice against bikers. You know the kind. Those that can't help but stare when a biker, man or woman, walks into the room. The sight of rugged jeans, tattoos, long goatees and black leather make outsiders look down their nose at bikers because they see a lower class of people. I'm ashamed to say that I used to be one of those outsiders. That was before I became a so-called biker babe and discovered a whole new world.

You know how kids, when they see motorcycles, they think it's the coolest thing in the world. They imagine what it would be like to ride one. One of my favorite movies growing up was, of course, *Grease*. When Michelle Pfeiffer sang "Cool Rider," I was right there with her, "looking for a dream on a mean machine with hell in his eyes." I would dance around my living room belting out the lyrics, "I want a C-O-O-L R-I-D-E-R." At the time, I thought everyone did that.

My fascination with motorcycles ended there. I didn't grow up hoping I would one day find a man who was "wild as the wind." In fact, three years ago, a pack of motorcycles could have pulled up next to me at a red light and I wouldn't have even heard the rumble of their engines. If by chance I did notice, I might look over, kind of down my nose, before disregarding them completely.

How foolish I was! Had someone told me they had the secret to escape this thing called life, I wouldn't have believed it, not in a million years. I now know differently.

When I first met my ex-boyfriend, Frank, I had no idea he was a biker. You know how you just look at someone and know that you belong together? That's how it was. When I found out he had a Harley, though, I figured I would use that to get his attention. The first thing I ever said to him was, "So, I hear you have a Harley." He responded with a "yup." That's when I said, "I've never been on a motorcycle before." What could he do, other than ask me if I wanted to go for a ride sometime.

The first time I saw Frank in his biker gear, with the boots and leather vest filled with pins and patches, I thought he looked silly. The first time we went for a ride, I wanted to wear my hair down with my cute shorts and a pair of sandals. That was before my hair knotted and the hot chrome pipes on his '96 1200 Sportster melted my sandal and burnt my leg. After that, I was ready for a ponytail, boots and jeans.

I am scared to death of airplanes, but the first time I rode on the back of Frank's cycle, I felt like I was flying. It was a rush of fear, excitement and freedom all rolled into one. I loved it! The bike thundered down the road, the engine roared and the wind blew my face so hard that when I tried to talk, saliva flew out of my mouth and across my cheek. I remember driving down this open road and Frank just put his hand out and moved it along the horizon to point out the sky stretched out in front of us. What a sight! It was amazing. I never imagined the sky and the sunset could look so different from the view of a motorcycle. The world felt more open, like nothing could touch me. Every time we went for a ride after that, it was like an adventure.

That's when I became an official biker babe. Or at least, that's what Frank called me. I wanted my own helmet and a leather vest. I even wanted to do the biker hand wave when other cycles went by. We went to all different bike meets and I loved walking around, looking at all the different motorcycles. There were so many different styles. Saddle bags, handle bars, sissy bars, seats, even tires. My favorite, without a doubt, were the unique fuel tank designs. It was so interesting to look at them, knowing that each one had a story of its own and somehow shed light on the person whose bike it was on.

It was at meets like these and different runs that I met people who belonged to a world I knew nothing about. They were all intimidating in some way. Whether they had the rough and tough scruffy look or were covered in tattoos, they were intimidating. But it didn't take long for me to realize that, in a way, they were no different than me. Sure they had a different lifestyle, but that didn't make them any less of a person than me or anyone I knew. Don't get me wrong, I did come across some bikers that really were rough and tough and mean, but so are many people who have never even been on a motorcycle.

Sandy was a supervisor where I worked. She had long, straight hair and fair skin. She hardly ever wore make-up. In fact, she never wore lipstick, only chap stick. The best way to describe her is plain and simple. She was a sophisticated woman in her thirties. Every day, she'd dress in a professional pants or skirt suit and low heels. I would have never pegged Sandy for a biker, but to my surprise, she was. It amazed me to find out that this petite, 5'2" woman rode one of those steel machines all by herself. Every now and again she would ride her bike into work on casual Friday. Her biker gear wasn't as extreme as Frank's or some others that I had met, but you definitely knew she was a biker.

Sandy and Frank introduced me to the ABATE (Alliance of Bikers Aid Toward Education) Toys for Tots run in Philadelphia. They both take part in the run every year. It was an event I had heard much about before I actually went, but still wasn't sure what to expect. Before my boyfriend and I went to the toy store, I bought a Barbie doll and he bought some kind of G.I. Joe, or something like that. As we headed over the bridge from New Jersey to Pennsylvania, I was amazed to see hundreds of cycles headed the same way. What was more amazing was all the toys that were strapped onto each and every bike.

This past year, more than 60,000 bikers took part in the run. With Santa in the lead, a sea of motorcycles headed out from Delaware Avenue towards the Children's Hospital. Once there, we parked the bikes and lined up, toys in hand, waiting to go into the hospital. The line stretched for more than a mile. Each biker walked through the hospital, one by one, and dropped his or her toy into one of the dozens of huge bins as all the kids, many in wheelchairs, watched and waved as they went by. What a sight! My description could not possibly do it justice. It was amazing and probably the coolest thing I've done in my life so far.

At that point, I couldn't understand how these people got such a bad reputation. Was it simply because of the way they looked? I realized that the answer to that was yes. I know how I used to view bikers, and that was based solely on appearances. It made me realize what a shame it is that we live in a world where there are stereotypes and that people of all walks of life can fall so easily into one category, regardless of who they really are.

For me personally, I'll never make that mistake again. I don't want to ride a bike myself. I don't think I have the courage. But it's funny, now when I meet a guy, I find myself wondering if he has a motorcycle, even hoping that he does. Now, a motorcycle could be far off in the distance and I hear it. I hear the roar of the engine long before I actually see the bike. I can even tell the difference between Harley Davidsons and the sporty Japanese bikes. Now, my head always whips around when a cycle thunders by. In fact, when a pack or just one pulls up next to me at a red light, I still look over and stare through my car window. I stare long and hard; only now it's not out of prejudice. It's out of pure jealousy.

Remember Strunk and White's advice to keep your writing simple and orderly? Here's how a professional writer followed the advice, and added a large dose of creativity in a conversational style.

"Close Encounters"
by Richard Panek
(reprinted by permission of **Natural History,** *September,* **2000;** *copyright the* **American Museum of Natural History, 2000)**
Asteroids have been getting a bad rap of late, which is better than the rap they used to get, which was none at all. But several developments in the past few

months—including fresh data from a spacecraft's visit to one asteroid and now the nightly appearances of another—have fostered a new interest in asteroids among professional and amateur astronomers alike.

Ever since January 1, 1801, when Italian monk and astronomer Giuseppe Piazzi discovered a relatively small celestial object he later christened Ceres, asteroids have been the orphans of the solar system—planets without portfolio. Maybe they were pieces of a planet that never quite coalesced. Maybe they were pieces of a planet that did coalesce but at some later point suffered a catastrophic collision. Maybe they were pieces of neither, but simply an odd assortment of space rocks left over from the solar system's birth and swept over time into the gap between the orbits of Mars and Jupiter by the give-and-take of gravity.

Maybe "maybe" doesn't belong in the scientific vocabulary—though in the case of asteroids, astronomers were willing to make an exception. There seemed to be no end to the number of asteroids, and no compelling reason to seek one. Occasionally an observer would stumble across a new asteroid, name it (often after a spouse, friend, or pet), and then pretty much forget about it. In 1887, a Scottish astronomer thought he'd found a new star, only to realize he'd rediscovered an asteroid that had first been sighted 80 years earlier. In 1916, U.S. astronomers Seth Nicholson and Harlow Shapley discovered a new asteroid (which they named after Shapley's wife, Mildred), only to lose it for much of the rest of the century (it resurfaced in 1991).

Today the state of asteroid knowledge can still be as spotty as the sky during a meteor shower. Most meteorites, in fact, are fragments of asteroids; astronomers can now say at least that much with certainty. But ask how many asteroids there might be out there, and the estimates range from hundreds of thousands to billions. Ask whether any of the asteroids that are not part of the main belt between Mars and Jupiter might be on an eventual collision course with Earth, and the answer is even less precise. Nobody knows.

Thanks to Hollywood's special-effects artists, as well as to an astronomer's mistaken prediction a couple of years ago that an asteroid could potentially be heading for an impact with our planet some 30 years hence, it's the apocalyptic possibilities of asteroids that have most captured the popular imagination. For scientists, however, these minor planets have begun to ignite a different kind of speculation: What if at least some asteroids are remnants of the primordial solar system?

Last February the spacecraft NEAR *Shoemaker* entered a close orbit with the asteroid Eros, specifically to investigate this possibility. Still, nobody at NASA had dared hope for what happened on May 4. For half an hour, while instruments on the NEAR tracked the 21-mile long asteroid from a distance of only 31 miles, a flare from the Sun washed over Eros, causing its elements to radiate X rays—and, in the process, to reveal the asteroid's chemical composition. Preliminary results show a collection of magnesium, silicon, and aluminum that has never undergone the kind of intense heating and melting that would characterize the development of a more mature terrestrial body. Therefore, Eros is indeed very likely a relic from the first stage of the solar system's formation.

That's not true of all asteroids, however, and one prominent exception has been visible in the night sky in recent months. Spectroscopic studies of Vesta during the 1990s revealed that lava once flowed on its surface, which means that this rather massive asteroid is a kind of cousin to Earth. With its diameter of approximately 335 miles, Vesta is the third-largest asteroid in the main belt. It is also the only main-belt asteroid occasionally seen with the naked eye by observers on Earth.

As September begins, Vesta is wrapping up a four-month period of such visibility. For the first few days of the month, in the hours just after nightfall, it will be shining in the southern sky at magnitude 5.8—just about the limit of our unaided viewing capabilities. From about September 7–19 it will wash out in the glare from the Moon, but when Vesta returns, it will be appearing near a reasonably conspicuous marker in the sky: the 5.5-magnitude star SAO 188192. Although by that time you'll need binoculars to see Vesta, careful monitoring should reveal the asteroid moving against the background stars from one night to the next.

Vesta won't be visible to the naked eye again until February 2003. Until then it may be out of sight but, like asteroids themselves these days, no longer out of mind.

HANDS ON

1. If you have not already done so, discover one or two writers of magazine articles whose work you especially admire, not so much for the subjects they write about, although that preference should not be discounted, but more for their style: the way they use words and construct sentences and paragraphs. Read them regularly; allow their artfulness to permeate your brain cells so that, gradually, their skill becomes yours as well.

   • Select from the magazines you like to read (but include one or two trade publications) good examples of how writers have employed direct quotation, narration, and anecdotes.

   • Select from the same magazines or others good examples of how writers have developed characters and scenes through expert and specific description.

2. You have likely already conducted one or more interviews. Revisit your notes and/or any articles based on those interviews. See if you could now make better use of direct quotation and whether you could more expertly blend direct quotation with narration.

   • Reexamine your previous writing and decide if you missed any opportunity to seek out and use an anecdote or case history that would enliven your prose and also help your reader better understand the points you are trying to make.

   • Reexamine previous writing to determine if you missed any opportunity to more fully develop characters or scenes. Either from your notes or recall, try to revise your writing by inserting more specific description of people and their surroundings.

CHAPTER

9

Rewriting and Editing

Rewriting and editing are not something you do after writing with the help of computer spelling and grammar checks. They are integral acts of the writing process.

Almost all writing divides into these five stages:

Stage 1: Testing several ideas and deciding on one. You now have direction for the next step.

Stage 2: Collecting information to put flesh on your bare-bones idea. In other words, research.

Stage 3: Organizing information. Deciding where the writing begins and ends and what goes in the middle.

Stage 4: Composing the manuscript.

Stage 5: Rewriting and editing.

Regard Rewrite as Part of the Writing Process

You need to concentrate on Stage 5 at this point. The first thing to say about rewriting is that the process calls for a review of ALL the previous stages. Ah, here's the rub. Rewriting does not mean a simple run through the manuscript looking for (and hoping you don't find) an occasional bad sentence, misspelling, or comma splice. It means asking yourself whether you have satisfied what you had in mind when you settled on your idea. Did it come out the way you planned? The review also means asking yourself if you have included all the information needed so that your reader will fully understand and appreciate your idea. Has the information been organized so that the idea is developed in an orderly, logical fashion. Lastly, you scrutinize the writing style to make sure you have expressed yourself in the best way possible.

Two men set out to write a book. The basic idea of the book was originally the brainstorm of one man; the second man was primarily the writer. Their modus operandi for composing the book began with an all-day session every other week where the idea man did most of the talking based on his knowledge and experience. He gave direction for each chapter. The sessions were taped. Then the writer downloaded the tape from each session, added information based on his own research and experience, and, finally, wrote a chapter.

At the start of the second session, the writer proudly handed chapter one to the idea man. The chapter ran to about 20 pages. The idea man, sitting in a comfortable chair, began to read while the writer nervously paced and kept one eye on his colleague to gauge his reaction to this well-honed paragraph or that precisely-crafted sentence. When the idea man finished reading, he looked up and said, "You are a very fine writer. This reads very well indeed." The writer glowed. "There's just one problem." Oh-oh, thought the writer, I made a boo-boo; some sentences don't sound right to him. "You missed the whole point of the book." In the comic strips, that's the point where the character who's hurting gags, "Aaaaarrrrggghhhh! " The writer's rewrite had not included a careful—often painful—reexamination of phase one of the writing process. He had not captured the basic idea.

Chapter one—all 20 pages of beautiful prose—was terminated.

Over the years, I often have pointed out the same fault to students: you lost track of your idea; perhaps you never had a firm grasp on it. Sometimes it turns out that the idea was simply not very good to begin with, and no matter how diligently the student worked on it, the idea never really took shape. It reminds one of a sculptor who has in mind to fashion a beautiful vase or figure, but he never succeeds because his clay is lacking in some way; it defies molding.

If, after an honest assessment of how well your idea has been developed (and every writer must be his first and most ruthless critic), you decide it didn't come off, do what the writer in the story had to do—start over.

Occasionally, your idea—the point of your story or the article's angle—may change in mid-writing. That is not necessarily a bad thing, except that the occurrence may mean that your research is wrong now, at least inadequate or off the mark. You have two choices—well, actually three. First, you can go back to your original idea in order to match your information to it. Option two is to conduct new research to fit your new idea. The third possibility, certainly not recommended, is to somehow muddle through, trying, so to speak, to plug your round research results into your square idea.

A professional writer met a woman who had survived the holocaust as a child in Poland. In fact, she had written a book about her experiences, especially how she had passed those terrible days by drawing pictures of what she imagined a child's life to be outside the room where she and her mother were hiding from the Nazis prowling the streets and houses looking to arrest and deport Jews. At the time the writer met the woman, she was lecturing schoolchildren about the holocaust and displaying her childhood art. She also was an eclectic collector of paintings, sculpture, theater posters and playbills, and other paraphernalia. In fact, her bathroom walls were papered in all manner of interesting materials. The writer queried a magazine, and the editor asked to see a finished article.

The writer is ordinarily very thorough in his rewrite, but this time he evidently paid scant attention to stage one, because the editor's response was that the article lacked focus. Indeed, she was correct. The writer's problem, which he should have picked up on during a reexamination of the idea stage, was that he had never decided what the article was all about. It wasn't clear whether he was writing primarily about the woman's World War II experience, her lectures to today's students, or her penchant for collecting unusual objets d'art. He made no sale.

Filling in Holes

Susan Carter, who wrote the article "Charlie 2–Drop! " (Chapter Eight) for her first assignment in the magazine article writing course, decided to write for her next assignment an article about a program that trains dogs to "hear" for deaf persons. After completing what she hoped was her final draft, she reviewed her work one last time. It is important to note, however, that she was still in the writing mode; rewrite is merely a final step in the writing process. The hole that was there in the article all along now loomed like a giant cavern. The director of the program had described to Carter how a family pet, a Chihuahua named Mouse, who had only started her training, ended up saving the family when they were in danger from leaking gas in the house. "Why didn't I interview family members?" Carter asked herself. The account of the rescue told in the words of the people involved would be much more thrilling and explicit than the program director's brief explanation of the incident, Carter correctly reasoned.

What she learned, of course, was that rewrite also means reconsidering whether the article has been thoroughly researched, whether enough information—or the right information—has been collected to make the article not only accurate but also as interesting at it should and could be.

Sometimes a review of stage two can be very painful and may cause the writer to either abandon the project altogether or result in considerably more research than the writer had bargained for. When student Ken McFarlane first began his article "Things You Can't Leave at Home," he thought he had a good idea—a good angle—and he was right. He spent a couple of weeks in Australia and noticed how American culture seemed to overshadow—even displace—local culture and how young Australians his age both resented and embraced the invasion. As he got into the article, and especially after he reviewed his best draft and commenced rewriting it, he realized that the export of American culture throughout the world—not just to Australia—was a huge and very complex subject. To do justice to the subject, even in a small way, would require substantially more research than he was able to accomplish. He changed and considerably narrowed the focus of his article.

Danger, Out of Order

You may recall your teacher of composition talking about coherence within and between paragraphs. The point of the lecture was that your writing must move logically from one thought to another, from explanation to example and not the other way around. During the rewrite stage, you should be looking for spots where sentence, paragraph, or whole section is out of order. The guts of your article may have to be reorganized.

Here are several examples of where information should have been rearranged for clarity:

An article about male cheerleaders in the National Football League focused in the beginning on how one male cheerleader related to his female colleagues. All very interesting, but first the reader should have been told about the role of male cheerleaders, especially since they are almost never seen when TV cameras zoom in on the pep squad. One could imagine the reader asking himself over and over again, "But what is that guy doing with all those girls anyway?" The primary reason he is there is not to be a diversion for female viewers, but to supply the biceps needed for demanding physical routines.

A student once wrote about the importance of the battle of Trenton on Christmas Day in 1776, when the flame of American independence was in danger of being snuffed out. The article described in great detail the battle and how it was the first victory recorded by Washington's Continental Army. It was nearly at the end of the article, however, before the reader learned what desperate straits the Continental Army was in that winter. Because of short-term enlistments, most of the soldiers Washington had were due to go home after January 1. That piece of information was critical to understanding why Washington chose to gamble everything—why his army either had to attack the Hessian garrison or dissolve, and possibly the new nation along with it.

Writers of how-to articles and other pieces that depend on a series of steps, explanations, or directions must, during the rewrite stage, carefully review those series to ensure the order is correct. The danger is that, in the original writing of the article, when information and sentences are flowing (as indeed they should), items in a series can be inserted as they occur to the writer. Because of this natural process, some items may be in the wrong order; still others may be left out. Stage five is where you see the problem and rearrange the series as necessary.

Remember What Mark Twain Said

A student, questioned about her choice of word, replied, "I really like that word." A pretty poor reason for using it. Mark Twain reminded all writers: "The difference between the right word and the almost right word is the difference between lightning and the lightning bug." In the rewrite/editing phase, one of a number of things you should do is to reexamine your choice of words and expressions. They do matter. In the final draft of the article "I Was a Biker Babe Once" (Chapter Eight), after Desiree Dunne talked about how she once looked down her nose at bikers, she began the next paragraph with this sentence: "How foolish was I?" During a careful review of the composition stage, she changed the question to an exclamation: "How foolish I was! " The difference is not slight. By asking the question, she in effect petitions the reader for judgment on her prejudice. However, when two words are reversed, she is scolding herself—condemning her own bias.

When Theodore Bernstein was assistant managing editor of the *New York Times,* he published an internal bulletin for staffers called "Winners & Sinners." Each issue included excerpts from some articles and headlines in recent editions of the *Times* that were very good and some that were not so good. Bernstein later published some of the best and worst in a book titled *Watch Your Language* (Channel Press, 1958). He had this to say near the close of the book's introduction:

"If writing must be a precise form of communication, it should be treated like a precision instrument: It should be sharpened and it should not be used carelessly. A book of instruction for use of this device would suggest to the writer that he choose the exact word, the one that flies straight to the target, rather than the diffuse word that hits other things besides the target; that he place each word where it will do its job best; that he construct his sentences so that they are tidy and logical; that in general he observe the grammatical practices that over the long years have bestowed continuity and orderliness upon the language."

Bernstein is not talking about proofreading. To proof a manuscript is primarily to look for typographical errors: a word that has been misspelled or has letters transposed (for example, braed instead of bread), their instead of they're, it's instead of its, misplaced or missing punctuation, and so on. While these kinds of errors can adversely affect or interfere with reading, they usually do not greatly alter understanding and meaning.

Bernstein and this chapter are talking about rereading sentences you wrote perhaps in haste or ignorance or sloppiness and exclaiming softly or out loud, "What the hell am I trying to say here! " Sentences like this one:

"Autonomy is defined as an individual's freedom to divert in intimate or private activities without the interference of regulations from the government."

Or this one:

"Children are born every year with debilitating defects that will have a cause on them for the rest of their life."

These sentences were allowed to stand by college students who have completed twelve or more years of schooling. They obviously have yet to learn what it means to rewrite and edit stage four—where composition takes place.

"Some writers have trouble revising because they become too attached to their own words," wrote Robin A. Cormier in her book *Error-Free Writing*, which is directed at those persons who write for business/trade publications. "They are reluctant to look for problems because finding them will only lead to more work, so they review their material quickly, with one eye closed. Other writers are never satisfied with what they have written and will continue to revise and revise and revise again until someone finally yanks the document out of their hands. Obviously, you should aim for somewhere in between. Nobody ever writes a perfect document on the first try, but you do have to let go eventually."

But don't let go until you have examined your article not with "one eye closed" but with the wide open eyes of your eventual reader. One hopes that the students who wrote those befuddled and muddled sentences above would, upon careful rereading, rewrite them so that they make sense to the reader.

Rewrite/Editing Checklist

Here is a checklist that might be helpful:

- ✓ Check clarity. Sometimes, the writer forgets that what is perfectly clear to him will not be clear to his reader unless he provides sufficient information, explanation, and definition.
- ✓ Check coherence and unity. Be sure paragraphs are focused and words, phrases, clauses, and sentences follow in logical order. Also, be sure you have provided necessary transitions between paragraphs.
- ✓ Check simplicity. Readers can be confused (and turned off) by overly long, complex sentences. If you find a sentence containing—juggling—two or more ideas or points, separate it into two or more sentences. (Clues to complexity: several semicolons followed by such transitional words as also, therefore, and moreover.)
- ✓ Check voice and tone. Remember, most magazine writing is conversational. However, depending on the subject, you may wish to sound authoritative (not know-it-all). Be sure you are coming across in the voice and tone you intended. Also, be sure you have used primarily active voice.

✓ Check direct quotation and paraphrase. Be sure direct quotation is accurate and properly attributed. Also, it is important that paraphrase and summary of source material are in your own words and proper credit has been given.

✓ Check consistency. For example, if you decided to write in first person and present tense, don't switch in mid-article to third person and past tense unless you have some valid reason for doing so. Also, be consistent in format. If, for example, your article started out as a how-to piece with one step following another, don't alter that format and confuse your reader.

Proofreading Your Article Draft

Your computer may have tools that check spelling and grammar. However, be forewarned (unless you have already been burned) that grammar checks are frequently questionable and sometimes downright wrong. Therefore, have at your side a standard grammar handbook in addition to a dictionary and the-saurus. And consult the handbook often.

Here are two problem areas that require particularly close and careful proofreading:

The preposition syndrome.   Prepositions number about 45 (there's one). For some reason that no one can fathom, high school and college classrooms are in the midst of a kind of preposition crisis. That is, teachers see more frequently than in past years student writing where the wrong or inappropriate preposition is used. Now, to be perfectly frank, the rules governing prepositions are not very exact. Indeed, the once hard-and-fast rule that decreed no sentence could end with a preposition has been scrapped. As much as anything, the student writer has to rely on common sense and on the way she has seen professional writers use prepositional phrases. While the problem is still in a sub-epidemic stage, you should pay special attention during proofreading.

Consider the following two sentences from student articles:

- "There are many things that can cause damage of hair structure."
- "This way the dog could alert the man of sirens. . . ."

The problem is the preposition "of." In both sentences, actions occur that affect someone or something. To put it another way, something is being done to something else. Hence, a common sense rule: In such an instance, use the preposition "to." The sentences above, then, would read as follows:

- "There are many things that can cause damage to hair structure."
- "This way the dog could alert the man to sirens. . . ."

Here's another example from student writing:

"What a charter school offers a student makes good competition or accountability on the regular public school system."

The preposition "on" usually is reserved for phrases related to placement: the book is on the table, he lives on Easy Street, she put on the sweater. The charter school, in this instance, is not putting competition on other public schools. It is assigning or giving something over to other public schools. Someone is providing something for someone else. The most appropriate preposition in such instances would be "for": "What a charter school offers a student makes good competition or accountability for the regular public school system." In the case of this particular sentence, it probably should be rewritten entirely.

The comma dilemma.   Think of punctuation as road signs. The period tells the reader to come to a complete stop before proceeding, perhaps in another direction. The semicolon is a go slow sign; the reader is coming to an important intersection of two thoughts. Commas are signs that advise about special conditions. But instead of alerting drivers to a hospital zone, cattle crossing, or detour, commas tell readers to watch out for a parenthetical clause, nonrestrictive phrase or series of things. The problem with some students' articles is (1) too many commas, (2) too few commas, or (3) commas in the wrong places.

Here are common comma faults:

• Comma separating subject and predicate. Consider this sentence: "I am a 22 year-old female, employed by the _____car wash." A comma never separates a subject from its predicate unless commas have been used for a nonrestrictive or parenthetical phrase describing the subject. An example would be as follows: "I am a 22-year-old female, slim and fastidious, employed by. . . ."

• Comma missing after an introductory clause. When a sentence begins with an adverb clause (such as this one), it is almost always followed by a comma (as in this case). Typically, adverb clauses start off with such words as after, although, because, if, since, when, and while. They modify—add information about—a verb. In our sentence above, the "when" clause modifies the verb "followed." In the sentence below, where the student initially left out the comma, the adverb clause modifies the verb "selling" in this sentence immediately preceding it: "Selling these items serves as an artistic outlet while making a small profit."

"While this type of thing can be found at any concert the bands Phish and Grateful Dead are the only concerts that really encourage it."

• Comma splice. Remember, the comma is a road sign; it tells the reader about little side detours into subordinate clauses and such. What it can't do is separate independent clauses—clauses with a subject and predicate that could stand alone as sentences. That's the job of periods and semicolons. Also, by itself it can't join two independent clauses. When a writer uses a comma alone to separate or join two independent clauses, that's called a comma splice. Here are a couple of examples from students' article drafts:

"It's not difficult, all you need is a little inspiration backed up by some hard work."

"The arts are forms of understanding and ways of knowing that are fundamentally important to education, children and youths who receive instruction in the arts and humanities . . . remain in school longer and are more successful than children who do not receive such instruction."

In both instances, the comma is incorrectly used to separate two independent clauses. In the first example, primarily because the two clauses are short and quite dependent on each other, a semicolon could be substituted for the comma. In the second example, however, the two clauses are quite long. Also, while they are about the same general subject, they don't depend on each other for meaning to the same degree as the two in the first example. One could still exist without the other. The most appropriate punctuation in this case would be a period.

Sometimes, the comma splice can be unspliced by including a coordinating conjunction after the comma (for example, and, but, for, and so). Here is an example where that was done: "The arts are integral to every person's daily life, and there is ample evidence that the arts help students. . . ."

When One Pass Is Not Enough

Most editors recommend to writers they make two or more passes through their manuscript when proofreading. In each pass, the writer looks for a particular problem or set of problems. This is especially helpful if you have a weakness that you want to catch and correct. For example, if you frequently misplace or omit commas, one run through might be devoted to that problem. Perhaps you are never sure when to use "whom" instead of "who," and you sometimes write "where" when you mean "were." Set one pass aside to look for those little faults.

Keep in mind when proofreading that your writing must conform to the magazine's preferences and requirements insofar as capitalization, abbreviations, persons' titles, numbers, and so on. Most publications adhere to the *Associated Press Stylebook,* and it would be a good idea for you to get your own copy (available in most college bookstores). For example, if you begin a sentence with a number, it should be written out; otherwise, numbers one through nine are spelled out and numbers 10 and over are written as numerals. Persons' titles generally are capitalized when preceding their name, but are not when they follow the name or stand alone. For example, "President Bush spoke at the event," but "The president spoke at the event."

FOR EXAMPLE

Deborah Barcan's article "The Edisons' Country Estate" (*Victorian Homes,* February 2001) begins by stating what she had in mind when setting out to write the article about the large Victorian home in West Orange, New Jersey. The house, she wrote, "represents the vision of four people: Architect Henry Hudson Holly, original owner Henry C. Pedder, and Thomas and Mina Edison, who infused it with life and brought it fame." In the article, she discusses, in order, Hudson's design, what Pedder did to the house, and how the Edisons placed their stamp upon it. The article is always true to the writer's initial intent.

In his article "Escape to the woods" (*General Store,* Winter 2000/01), John Runyon advocates weekend hiking and camping in the winter. In organizing the points he wants to make about this adventure, he's careful to select as point number one what is most critical for the winter hiker to understand and follow: "The first step to take, hopefully well before the Friday night previous to departure, is to gather clothes and equipment you already have available. Find all the lightweight wool, fleece, and polypropylene clothing you can."

Douglas H. Chadwick, along with photographer David Doubilet, explored Australia's Great Barrier Reef and wrote about the adventure in the January 2001 issue of *National Geographic* ("Kingdom of Coral"). While much of his article is devoted to vivid descriptions of the spectacular beauty of the reef and its denizens, Chadwick is careful to insert in just the right places the fruits of his careful research, information the reader needs to know for better understanding. Early on in the article, for example, he writes:

"Coral reefs form when colonies of tropical marine plants and animals with limestone skeletons rise atop earlier generations. They fashion the most visually diverse natural environments a human can experience, and the Great Barrier Reef is the world's single largest coral domain. With the broad, shallow continental shelf of tropical northeastern Australia providing an ideal pedestal for growth, this coral complex reaches as far as 160 miles offshore and more than 1,250 miles from north to south. The Great Barrier Reef covers 135,000 square miles, an expanse greater than Poland."

The article "The Iraq Factor" by Nicholas Lemann in the January 22, 2001 issue of *The New Yorker* contains this sentence: "A business coalition called USA-Engage is pressing for the abolition of economic sanctions against some anti-American regimes (Iran, for example); Bush can't make that call without making either business or the right angry." One doesn't know, of course, what Lemann's earlier drafts looked like, but this is the kind of construction that could cause some student writers problems. On first run-through, the inexperienced writer might easily insert a comma where the semi-colon is and create a comma splice—try to separate two independent clauses with a comma. During stage five—revise and rewrite—is when the student might have to choose between leaving the comma splice, substituting the semicolon, inserting a period between the two clauses, or joining the two clauses with the conjunction "but."

H A N D S   O N

1. Review in a standard writing handbook any subject areas that regularly give you trouble. If you are one of those persons suffering from the preposition syndrome, examine the section on prepositions; if you've had an ongoing dilemma about comma placement, reread the chapter on punctuation. Resolve to no longer tolerate recurring errors in grammar, word choice, sentence construction, punctuation, or spelling—because editors won't.

   - As you read articles in your favorite magazines, be more conscious of how writers construct sentences. Apply the checklist that begins on page 128.

2. The passage below is badly in need of revision and rewriting. Be prepared to note omissions and errors; suggest revisions and correct errors as necessary.

   Don't rely on your computer's spelling and grammar checkers.

   New employees can now expect to undergo some forms of drug testing. Random testing of employees have become more common despite some recent court decisions.

   Testing was instituted beginning in the 1980s, employers reacted when government agencies and the media called attention on the growing number of cases of employees missing work or making costly errors on the job. Due to drug use.

   Many testing programs have been criticized because they may be unconstitutional. Critics argue that the tests don't consider as they certainly should whether or not the people undergoing the testing in the first place have been tested by they're employers because the employers have thought that the employees may have been using druges of some sort in the past, also they suspect the employees are still currently using drugs.

   While some early court cases, such as Lovvern v. City of Chattanooga, found unconstitutional the wide spread random testing of firefighters more recent court decisions have upheld random testing. One interesting case involved a trucking firm that argued it's testing policy was in accord with regulations under the federal highway administration of the department of transportation.

   Pauline Kale, Constitutional Lawyer, stated, "The constitution clearly views random testing based on random suspicion without grounds as being a infringement of individual rights, the question isn't arguable in my opinion."

10 Becoming a Freelance Writer

When her third child left home, after 30 years of marriage, and while working full time as a college librarian, Faye Robinson decided to take an undergraduate course in magazine article writing and become a freelance writer. So far, she hasn't had much success. That makes her almost the archetypical freelancer.

This is how she began her first article draft:

"The boy (man) was the last of the flock to fly away. Three of them took flight, taking only their 'good' things, leaving all their junk in the nest they wrecked. They left me with one thing intact, a stranger. My husband of 31 years was a stranger to me, and, if he would admit it, I was a stranger to him.

"[But] the three little birds who conspired against me, leaving an empty, wrecked nest did not know what a blessing it was for them to fly. Because there were some major repairs needed; my husband and I had to communicate—something we had not done for years unless it involved the children."

The article went on to describe how Robinson and her husband repaired not only what needed fixing in the house, but also what needed fixing in their relationship. One outcome of both enterprises was the conversion of a storage room used by her husband into a writing room used by her.

Robinson queried three consumer magazines about the empty nest article and three others for a second article she wrote, that one based on off-the-wall questions students sometimes ask librarians (for example, "Where are the regular books; you know, books people read?"). She received encouragement from some editors but no acceptances.

The reasons Robinson is something of a model freelancer are these:

She started in mid-life. Not that all freelance writers are between 40 and 60. The point is that a person can become a freelancer at anytime in his/her life. There's no age limit, no expiration date.

She holds another job. Very few persons make a decent living as a freelance writer. Most fit writing into an otherwise busy schedule. Some freelancers work at their word processor very early in the morning, others very late at night.

She set aside space for writing. Admittedly, one could sit on the sofa in the TV room and compose on a laptop while other members of the family are watching "Wheel of Fortune." However, writing generally is a solitary—some would say lonely—undertaking requiring one's full and uninterrupted attention. A speaker at a writers' conference described some side activity writers might engage in, then quickly added, "Of course, we writers hardly need still another excuse for not writing." Everyone in the audience laughed, because at one time or another they all had invented some excuse for putting off writing. Going off to write, to sit facing a computer screen that stares back at you brightly and impatiently (if you don't start typing it will fade into screen saver), can be a daunting experience.

Robinson realized that if she was serious about writing she needed to find isolated space outfitted at least with a table for computer and printer, a comfortable chair to sit in, good lighting, and room to spread out notes and such resources as Strunk and White's *Elements of Style*. She fixed up a storage area, but space for writing can be designated almost anywhere. One freelance writer used a small alcove off a bedroom; another set up in a closed-in porch warmed in winter by a space heater; still another refitted a walk-in closet no longer used by anyone in the family.

She began by writing about personal experiences. You need to be very clear about this point. New writers have been advised for generations, too many to remember, to write about what they know best. Many persons interpret this bromide to mean that writers should write only or almost always about personal experience, what they understand from first-hand knowledge. This, however, is a too narrow interpretation. A better way to think about this age-old counsel is that the writer must know fully whatever subject he is writing about. In most cases, that knowledge comes from thorough research. While it isn't a bad idea for a novice freelancer to write initially from personal experience, she shouldn't limit herself to that genre.

Robinson queried several magazines at once. Unless your article idea is a perfect fit for only one publication (very unlikely), or you insist (unwisely) on seeing your byline in only one of the premier magazines, you should query two or three publications at the same time. You may want to tailor your article idea and query differently for each magazine (especially if you mix consumer and trade publications). Of course, a gamble or risk is involved. Suppose you first receive an acceptance from the magazine you least favor, or the one that doesn't pay as well as the others, you must decide whether to submit your article to that magazine or decline (at least delay) acceptance and hope for an assignment from another editor.

Finally, her two ideas were rejected by all editors. Many freelance writers, unless they are established contributing writers for only one magazine, can paper at least a wall of their work room with rejections—the majority of them form letters cranked out by the dozens or hundreds. Some years ago, a cartoon titled "Why The Dinosaurs Perished!" showed a dinosaur looking bug-eyed at a letter from an editor that read, "Thank you for letting us consider the enclosed manuscript. Although it has obvious merit, we are sorry to say that it does not suit our present needs."

Robinson was so discouraged by the rejections that she hesitated submitting any more ideas to editors. A big mistake! If you're going to try your hand at freelance writing, you must expect many of your article ideas to be turned down. The problem may be with your idea or with your query letter. The primary reason why an article idea is rejected is because the writer didn't know the magazine and its readers very well; the idea simply didn't belong at that particular publication. But editors reject ideas for other reasons: an article about the same or a similar topic ran within the last year or two, or the magazine currently has a backlog of ideas and articles.

Improve Your Odds

Most American magazines rely mostly on freelance writers to fill their pages. The guidelines that follow may help you become a better freelance writer with a better chance of getting published.

Specialize.   Never ignore a good idea for an article, regardless of subject, but you probably will fare better in the long run if you focus most of your writing in one or perhaps two subject areas. The advantages of such specialization are these:

You can write mostly about a subject that interests you. Suppose, for example, you are a runner. Many persons share your interest. The *1999 Bacon's Magazine Directory* lists 19 consumer and trade publications about running. Also, a quick search of the Internet showed a fairly extensive number of www running links. These print and online publications explore running from many different angles. For example: running as a professional, collegiate and scholastic sport; running for health and exercise; running gear, etc.

You may become a recognized authority in your field, Lee Beadling (who wrote the article "Man With the Baby") is now a freelancer who specializes in health and medicine, but particularly in the area of orthopedics. When he graduated from college, he took a job as a staff writer for *Orthopedics Today.* He had no background in the subject and, at the time, no special interest. Beadling wanted to write, and, like most college graduates, he wanted a job (in his case, being married and a new father, he *needed* a job). He learned about orthopedics by attending conferences for orthopedists and listening to their speeches, reading their papers, asking them questions, and consulting such references as *Dorland's Medical Dictionary.* He wrote eight hours a day, five days a week about new research and treatments and reported news out of governmental and other agencies that affected orthopedists.

Says Beadling: "I finally got to be known and respected by orthopedists [some even asked him to help write their speeches]. Also, because *Orthopedics Today* is the only magazine of its kind, the mainstream media reporters sometimes call me as a source." Beadling is still writing regularly for that magazine as a freelancer; he also writes for some other publications connected to orthopedics. For example, if laboratory research should find that high heels somehow affect the ankle and leg bones of the wearer, the sponsor of the research may want Beadling to write an article about the research for the general press.

As a specialist, you not only become known to those who work regularly in your adopted field, but you also become known to editors of publications in the subject area. In fact, editors may approach you to write for their publication instead of the other way around. Robert Stowe England, for example, is in that position. He specializes primarily in business, finance, and the economy. "I had no training or experience in the field," he says, "but I became interested in it when I took a position as an editor for *Delaware Valley Business* magazine in 1976." Today, editors of such publications as *Mortgage Banking, Banking Strategies,* and *Financial World* frequently contact England and suggest article ideas for his consideration. He believes he is sometimes sought out by editors precisely because he has had no formal training in business and does not come from the ranks of bankers and financiers. "I bring a fresh perspective. I'm not a mortgage banker; I'm a journalist."

Keep an idea file.   Whether or not you specialize, you should maintain folders containing article ideas. The folders might contain clippings of stories from newspapers, magazines, and newsletters; notes you've jotted down after watching a show on television; something you downloaded from the Internet; notes from casual conversations or more structured interviews with interesting and knowledgeable people; or any idea that has occurred to you. Some writers keep a pad or cassette recorder by their bed because they sometimes wake up in the middle of the night with a brainstorm and they don't want to forget it.

Periodically go through the folders and decide what among the contents still interests you and has remained timely. Consider, then, what would be required of you to develop the ideas into query letters and what magazines are most likely outlets for an article. Here are two actual examples of how this system works:

A freelance writer attended a concert by a choir of Hispanic teenagers from an urban ghetto. He was impressed and moved by the quality of their singing. He asked a few questions of the choir director after the performance and jotted down notes on the concert program. Some months later, he was going through his file and came across the program. He wrote a query to *Vista Magazine,* a Sunday supplement magazine like *Parade* that appears in major newspapers serving a large Hispanic population. The editor bought the idea and, later, the article and pictures.

While browsing through his local newspaper, a freelance writer was intrigued by an article about a man whose hobby was blowing intricate glass figures, something of a lost art today. He clipped the article and placed it in his file—and forgot about it. Almost a year later, the writer was talking to a publisher who was about to launch a new magazine. The publisher said he was thinking about including an occasional piece about people with unusual and interesting hobbies. "Do you know of anyone like that?" was the publisher's question. You know the writer's answer.

Maintain contacts with editors. Many freelance writers, particularly those new to the business (and it is a business), fail to take an editor seriously who closes a rejection letter with sentences such as the following lifted from real letters:

"Please consider sending other submissions."

"We would welcome the opportunity to see more of your work."

"I am sorry it [the article idea submitted] is not what we are looking for at this time, but I hope you will think of us again soon."

Don't pester editors with a non-stop barrage of query letters containing hastily-contrived, unresearched ideas. But you should follow up such invitations with the occasional letter offering editors well-thought-out ideas that you honestly believe are right for their magazine. Make sure the letters are exceptionally well written. What you are telling editors is that you are a serious freelancer with good ideas and the skill needed to turn the ideas into lively, highly readable articles focused toward their audience.

Of course, it is especially important to keep in touch with an editor of a magazine that already has published an article by you. It is almost always easier to sell a second article idea to that editor than it was the first one. The reason is that the editor already knows several important things about you:

- Your writing style is compatible with the magazine's.
- You are apparently familiar with the magazine's audience.
- You are dependable. You accept and follow suggestions for rewrite, and you can meet a deadline.

Operate as a business. If you are a serious, part-time freelance writer, then you also should be a serious businessperson. That means you conduct yourself professionally, maintain an office atmosphere, supply yourself with the proper equipment and resources needed to work effectively and efficiently, and keep careful financial records.

When contacting sources or editors, always identify yourself as a freelance writer. You are not someone who decided on the spur of the moment to see if you could write an article. If you make contacts as a college student, still identify yourself as a freelance writer rather than as a student who has to write something to satisfy his professor's assignment. Use the language of the writer; be prepared to talk about queries, writing on spec, sidebars, bullets, and transparencies. When you keep appointments with sources or editors, dress appropriately. This does not mean you necessarily have to put on corporate clothes, but remember, first impressions do count.

Wherever you work, treat it as your office. This might mean that it is off limits to family members and pets when you are at work. It also means you do not listen to your favorite radio station or play CDs, and you don't flick on the TV or bring up a game on your computer. Basically, avoid placing anything in your work area that could distract you from the task at hand—writing.

In addition to the obvious equipment previously mentioned (table, chair, etc.), you probably should equip your work area with a telephone, audio cassette player, and, possibly, a fax machine. The audio cassette player is important if you record interviews, as most writers do. Buy a foot pedal that attaches to the machine. This way you can stop and start your cassette as needed and still have your hands free to transcribe.

If you are a serious freelance writer, you should keep close tabs on expenses and income, because you may be entitled to business deductions, and you may have to report business income. Depending on how serious you are, you may be able to deduct such expenses as depreciation on office equipment, business phone calls, travel expenses, and costs of mailing queries and articles. In certain situations, if you use a room (not a corner of a room or closet) primarily or exclusively for writing, you may be able to deduct a portion of utilities costs. For example, suppose your house consists of eight rooms, including a small bedroom you have converted into a work area. You may be entitled to deduct one-eighth of the annual costs of electricity, heating, and air conditioning.

The Internal Revenue Service does not dictate who qualifies as a serious freelance writer, nor does it spell out exactly how much writing you must attempt or accomplish during the year in order to qualify for deductions. You may assume, however, if you go to your computer only occasionally during the year and dabble with a few article ideas, you do not qualify as a serious writer entitled to deductions. Check with a tax adviser if you believe you might qualify.

Also, keep a record of your income; you may have to report payments for articles from one source that exceed a certain amount ($500 in the year 2000). The reason you may have to report the income is because the magazine that paid you may have to file an IRS form 1099 (you should receive a copy). The IRS may compare your return with that from the magazine that paid you. Here again, consult a tax adviser.

Working With Editors

If you submit a good article idea to a magazine and the editor likes it, you may assume that the editor wants to see the article published as much as you do (well, maybe not quite as much). At least the editor is willing to invest time, energy, and money into the effort to publish your article in the best light and most readable form possible. That's no small investment. Of course, you have invested a lot, too: time, energy, blood, sweat, and tears. You and the editor will have to work closely together, and both of you probably will have to give and take, with you possibly doing more of the taking, at least in the way of direction and advice.

The interaction begins when the editor tells you what length your article should be and comments on how the article might be developed. Very often, the editor also will send you the magazine's writers' guidelines. The guidelines usually describe the publication's audience in specific terms and include such general directions as "your article must be thoroughly researched." They also may describe requirements for specific sections or departments of the magazine. For example, the guidelines for articles about health in a women's or men's magazine may differ from those for articles about investing.

Pay attention to the editor's instructions. If you had in mind writing a feature of about 2,000 words and the editor assigns 750 words, your article better be very close to 750 words. The editor probably already knows what edition your article will appear in and may have decided where your piece will fit (perhaps even have set aside space in a page layout).

The editor very likely will suggest how the article should be developed based on your brief outline in the query letter. These suggestions, at least some of them, may be negotiable, but if your plans for development differ substantially from the editor's and you want to counter her points, make sure your position is reasonable and arguable. Keep in mind from the outset, of course, that the editor has the last word, unless your last word is to withdraw from the project.

Remember, too, that the editor at least knows her readers better than you do and knows how her magazine—and probably competing publications—may have treated the general subject of your article in the past (not necessarily your specific angle). The editor also has a feel for the magazine's writing style that you probably do not, at least not to the same extent. For example, your research has produced one good anecdote or case history, but you may not have picked up on the fact that most features in the magazine contain more than one anecdote or case history. Therefore, when the editor suggests your article should contain two or three anecdotes or case histories, it is because she wants your writing style to conform to the magazine's.

The interaction and mutual understanding between you and an editor becomes confusing and threatening to the successful publication of your article when either one of you—or both—are vague in your communication. An editor once assigned a freelance writer an article about exploring a state park. The writer assumed the editor primarily wanted him to hike trails and describe what he saw. The editor later rejected the article, claiming that she was looking for something else—a something else never clearly defined. This is an example of editor and writer not communicating clearly. The editor never defined exactly what she was looking for, and the writer never asked enough questions to pin down the editor.

If you've browsed through a guide book like *Writer's Market*, you probably have noticed in some of the listings a reference to a kill fee. What this means is that the magazine will pay the writer a percentage of the standard payment for an article if, for some reason, the assigned article is rejected, or otherwise not published. In another instance, an editor of a major magazine contacted a newspaper reporter and asked him to write a much longer feature for the magazine based on an article he had written for his newspaper. The reporter accepted the assignment and later turned in the article. The editor sent the article back with suggestions for rewrite (not an uncommon practice). The writer completed another draft and sent it to the editor. Again, the editor turned back the draft and told the writer what he thought was wrong with the article. The writer composed a third version of the article, but it was still not what the editor wanted. At that point both editor and writer agreed the project was not destined for success, and the magazine paid the writer a kill fee.

The problem was twofold. First, the writer was not sufficiently familiar nor comfortable with the magazine's writing style. He couldn't quite bridge the gap between the bang-bang newspaper style—short paragraphs and just enough words to briefly describe an action or make a point—and the magazine's style of full development, including longer and more literate sentences. Second, his research was enough for the newspaper piece, but nowhere near enough to support the much more extensive article desired by the magazine.

Both editor and writer, in this case, tried to communicate clearly with each other, but to no avail. It can happen. Again, the editor has the last word; it must be so.

A major misconception on the part of many young freelance writers is that a magazine's editorial staff has both the time and patience to work with them, perhaps even to complete the rewriting and proofreading for them. Perhaps the notion derives in part from the writer's experience in school and college, where many teachers take the time to meticulously go over a student's work sentence by sentence, suggesting changes and correcting errors in grammar, punctuation, and spelling. Add to this the vision many writers have of a magazine's editorial office: a floor full of editors, associate editors, and editorial assistants all prepared to spend as much time with writers and their work as the writers desire. The fact is that most editorial offices, even in the case of some major publications, function with a very small staff, often consisting of no more than the editor, managing editor (usually in charge of production), and perhaps a staff writer and editorial assistant. Many staffs are smaller than that.

It is nearly impossible, therefore, for an editor to give writers and their articles the individual attention the writers think they deserve. Thus, the burden is on you to perform the following tasks:

• Be specific about your article in your query letter and in any subsequent communication with the editor or his assistant concerning the article. If the editor asks you to explain or elaborate on some aspect of your query or article, be as precise as possible in your response. On the other hand, if instructions from the editor are not clear, don't pretend to understand if you don't; ask for clarification.

• Be exceedingly careful and thorough with your rewriting and proofreading. Do not expect the editor or his assistant to perform these functions for you. If you have agreed to write an article of 1,000 words and the piece prints out of your computer at 1,500, be responsible for cutting out 500 words. The editor does not have time to go through your article and decide where the slashing should take place. It is in your interest to control the rewriting and the cuts in any event.

• Be prompt in meeting deadlines. Ordinarily, you have only one deadline, but the editor is dealing with a number of them involving the total process of putting out the next edition and the one after that and the one after that.

Illustrating Your Articles

"State availability of photos with submission." That is a familiar line in the magazine listings in the *Writer's Market*. What follows that line usually is information about the kinds of photos wanted and whether the magazine pays extra for the photos or whether it pays the author a flat rate regardless of the number of photos submitted. The point is that many magazines want to illustrate articles with one or more pictures, and if the articles come from freelancers, the magazine expects them to also be illustrators.

When magazines speak of photos, generally they mean 2 × 2-inch color slides, called transparencies in the business. From the standpoints of quality reproduction and convenience, magazines generally prefer slides over color prints. However, sometimes color prints are the only photos available, and, in some cases, black and white photos might be preferred. For example, a freelance writer wrote an article about the first Jewish agricultural community in the United States, founded in the late 1800s. He supplied black and white photos showing life in the community at the turn of the century. The magazine used the photos and had them tinted a sepia tone, which made them look like what they were, old pictures from someone's dusty album.

If the magazine you are querying wants to know about photos and you do not have any available at the time, you can always advise the editor that photos can be supplied with the article, which means you or someone you designate will have to take them. Whether you already have photos or need to take them, they need to be of professional quality. Many persons take pictures; its very easy these days with the kinds of cameras that require not much more of the photographer than to point in the direction of the subject and push a button. But pointing and pushing doesn't necessarily guarantee that a quality photo will result. It is amazing to see, when attending an indoor concert or sports event, to see flashbulbs popping all over the hall, often from seats one-half mile from the performer or action. Flashbulbs are rarely effective more than 10 feet away.

However, lighting, while important to picture quality, is only one element to be considered. An even more critical concern is what the lens frames—the picture the photographer is going to get when the film is processed. A professional photographer advises that many persons, when they focus on the people or landscape they especially want to capture, forget to look carefully all around the periphery of the scene framed by the lens. For example, the photographer may be so busy making sure the subject of the photo is posed correctly that he fails to notice someone or something in the background that is distracting or inappropriate. A companion concern is the distance between the subject and the lens. Most magazines want photos which show the subject or action close up. This is contrary to the kinds of photos many amateurs take, where the subject or action is so far away that it blends into the extraneous background.

If you must supply photos for an article you have written and you don't consider yourself very accomplished or professional behind a camera, then you must find another way to acquire photos. Basically, you have only two choices: either obtain photos from some other source or engage a good photographer to take pictures for your article. In some cases, professional-quality slides already are available and you are allowed to use them or to make duplicate slides. In other cases, you may have to buy available photos. If you must have pictures taken, be careful of the arrangements you make with the photographer. First, agree on payment. If the magazine pays extra for photos, the photographer may be willing to supply photos for whatever the magazine pays and charge you only for the cost of film and processing. However, many professional photographers charge a hefty hourly or daily rate, and you will not come close to paying for their service out of the check you receive from the magazine. In either case, if you engage someone else to take pictures for you, even if he or she is a friend, you might do well to draft a simple agreement spelling out the terms.

Some magazines require you to supply a model release form for anyone appearing in your photos. You can make up the form. It should simply state two things: (1) the subjects agree to have their picture taken and reproduced in a publication—any publication without their further approval, and (2) they do not expect to be paid. Magazines are concerned (and you should be) that a subject of a photo might later come forward and say he didn't expect to look like he does and/or didn't think his face would appear in THAT magazine. The other concern is that a subject might come forward later and claim he was promised $100 if he posed for the picture.

Illustrations also come in other forms. For example: drawings, cartoons, charts, tables, graphs, and maps. You may not have to supply any of these things, but the editor may appreciate your suggesting what the magazine's graphics person(s) might compose. If, for example, the writer believes his article about the rising cost of prescription drugs for seniors would profit from a graph showing the increase over a 10- or 20-year period, he should offer that suggestion and supply the figures. He does not have to draw the graph (although that has become simpler to do because of computer software). For an article for *Motor Home* about traveling to various Revolutionary War sites, the writer suggested a road map and provided directions. While the magazine did not provide a detailed map, it did come up with an illustration that showed the general location of the sites.

Writing for Online Publications

Online publications have been discussed in previous chapters, but some additional tips here might be helpful as you consider freelance writing for online magazines.

Most articles in most online publications tend to be shorter than those in print magazines, even in the case of a magazine which publishes both print and online versions. Wrote Michael Ray Taylor in *Writer's Market 2000*, "Online readers may read several related pieces of 700 to 1,000 words, but they just don't have the patience for very long features; very few online magazines will now consider anything longer [than 700–1,000 words]. It's not so much that Internet readers have short attention spans (although that may be true of many), but the physical act of reading on a screen and scrolling with a mouse is simply more effort to most people than the comparable act of thumbing through a magazine on the couch or in bed."

Web sites go for links, which are both similar and dissimilar to sidebars in print publications. A link is similar to a sidebar in the sense that it is something related to the feature article. But it is, or can be, dissimilar because the link may take the reader to information in a form other than a short article, perhaps to graphics. And the link may even call attention to another web site. Taylor provides an example of a travel feature where one link takes the reader to another web site for information about companies that sponsor tours to the site of the travel feature. "In your initial query," Taylor wrote, "it is thus wise to suggest one to three Internet links for the average factual article. . . ."

Query an online publication via e-mail. Queries to online publications tend to be shorter and hipper than queries to print publications. Taylor calls online writing "informal, smart, often irreverent. In short, online writing is playfully cool." If you're not sure what that means, you're not alone. "The Web is still in its infancy," wrote Taylor; "so far no one has figured out exactly what message its audience wants." As in the case of print publications, however, your best bet to figuring out what an online magazine's readers want is to read the magazine.

F O R   E X A M P L E

Emily Willingham of Austin, Texas wrote the following letter about her freelancing career. It was published by Angela Adair-Hoy's WriteMarkets newsletter *WritersWeekly.com* June 15, 2000. Willingham, a doctoral student at the time, talks about specialization v. generalization, Internet research, professionalism, and getting along with editors.

> I'm just about to finish my Ph.D. in reproductive biology, but I also have an undergraduate degree in English. My biological knowledge ranges from human medicine to reptilian behavior to toxicology. My English career has involved teaching, public affairs, and an addiction to Victorian literature. What kind of a vocation can somebody carve from all that?
>
> Generalist freelance writer is one possibility. I started two years ago targeting queries on anything that I understood well, and waited—sometimes for months—to see what hit the mark. I suspected that the Web would be my oyster, and my first paid publication ever was a piece on taking the GRE—published at a helpful web site for people returning to college. I broke all the rules by submitting a completed manuscript by e-mail, and they accepted it in a day.
>
> Since then, I've parlayed my understanding of toxicology into an online feature in a prestigious science newsletter; my experience with fear of heights into a piece for *Backpacker* magazine; my knowledge of dogs into a cover story for *Dog Fancy,* and my lifelong interest in medicine into lucrative projects writing content for patient-oriented medical web sites. In addition, I have a regular gig as a—surprise!—generalist and health reporter for an online magazine for

people 50 or better. In the meantime, I've written a few travel pieces and had them published online and in our local paper. Even the unthinkable has happened to me—someone saw one of my pieces online and offered me regular work writing educational science articles for interactive web sites.

The usual advice is to find a niche, but I think my niche is whatever I find interesting. If I focused only on wildlife biology, I never would have had the pleasure of learning all about German Shepherds, and I wouldn't know everything I now understand about heart disease. As I continue to write, my focus narrows; for example, I've cut out most of my travel-writing efforts. But I still keep some special travel stories—like being struck by lightning in Yellowstone, heading out on a quest for the Great Wall in China, and crossing the Arctic Circle—in my mind in case I see a place for them.

I work full-time from my home and make a good living freelancing. One key to my success is the Internet. Become a crackerjack Internet researcher and the world is at your fingertips. And, of course, you'll find plenty of jobs for freelancers on the information highway. One of the greatest things I ever did for myself was to put up my web page (http://www.writingweb.net) and buy a professional-sounding (I hope) name for it. It's been an easy way for prospective editors to examine my work, look at my resume, and learn about me, and it's fun to be able to return regularly and update it with newly accepted publications.

One final characteristic I try to cultivate is complete professionalism with editors. My words are not carved in stone, and my attitude is that editors know best what works for their publications. So far, courtesy and professionalism have paid off. I've received second assignments from several publications, including *Backpacker.* My varied background has given me the tools to be able to say, "Yes" to many disparate assignments, and it has been a great way to build up a portfolio of samples for almost any field that interests me.

Roseann Brownell was a college senior when she queried *College Bound Magazine.* In response to Brownell's query, Gina LaGuardia, editor-in-chief, offered Brownell a contract and very specific instructions on how to write the article. The query letter and LaGuardia's response follow:

Dear Ms. LaGuardia:

It's one of their worst predators. Yet college students continue to fall prey to its incentives—low interest rates, free gifts, and quick cash. For some, however, the credit card is the beginning of a downward spiral into a land of never ending debt.

It would be much easier to survive college without falling into the debt hole if students were taught the ins and outs of credit cards before they even stepped foot on campus. Hopefully, my article will give high school seniors the insight needed to stay debt free by explaining how credit card companies target a college demographic and by also giving examples of students who were reeled into debt while in college.

Finally, a how-to on getting by financially without credit cards would be included. High school seniors would then be prepared to either save up money from a summer job, put extra spending money on their university's debit card, or open a bank account in which they could request a check card that would act as their credit card.

I am currently a senior at Rowan University in Glassboro, New Jersey. I have personally experienced the effects of credit card debt in college. This and my current studies in magazine article writing give me the experience needed to write such an article. If needed, I will be able to provide photos or artwork with my article.

Thank you for your consideration.

Sincerely,

Roseann Brownell

LaGuardia advised Brownell that her main article should be 700–1,000 words long, with at least two shorter sidebars. Under the heading Article Focus, LaGuardia gave these instructions:

"Your article should explore the intricacies of credit card spending amongst college-age students and discuss the myths and realities surrounding responsible (and irresponsible) credit card usage. As stated in your query, your article should focus on providing valuable how-to advice for starting out and staying financially sound as a college student, with or without a credit card. Include a real-life 'story of woe' and 'of prosperity,' uncover tips on how one can be a 'wise card user,' explore the warning signs of excessive use, etc. Supplement the article with some instructional sidebars: 'In over your head?', 'How to get help . . . ', etc. Be sure to consult college students and credit card/money management experts (recommended sources enclosed)."

Among the sources enclosed was a letter from Phoenix Home Life Mutual Insurance to LaGuardia describing a national survey of students aged 12 to 21 that revealed they "are unprepared to handle financial responsibility, but they are interested in learning about money management."

Many freelancers write for a mix of consumer, trade, and professional publications. The following article appeared in the Fall 1997 issue of the *Journal of Telecommunications in Higher Education* published by the Association of College and University Telecommunications Administrators.

"New Jersey's Cybercampus Brings New Structure to Education"
by Charles H. Harrison
New Jersey is less than two years away from linking most of its 563 public school districts, 46 colleges and universities, and dozens of public libraries in a giant communications network featuring distance learning, interactive television (ITV), teleconferencing, and the Internet.

That's the prediction of William Reynolds, Director of Instructional, Technical, and Media Services for the Division of Continuing Professional Education at New Jersey Institute of Technology (NJIT) in Newark. His institution plays a major role in the fast-paced drive to create a cybercampus for the nation's most densely populated state.

Fueling the effort is a $200-million state appropriation that enables each public and private college and university to fully equip at least one distance-learning classroom. Additional funding is allocated to schools through the Office of Technology in the state Department of Education. To date, the state has awarded Tele-Measurement Inc. of Clifton, New Jersey, contracts to equip distant-learning classrooms in 40 colleges and 22 high schools and technical schools. The company provides cameras, monitors, videotaping and audio equipment, master control panels, table microphones for student tables, and all electronic software, according to Bill Endres, President of Tele-Measurement. Tele-Measurement has also installed ITV equipment in an additional 160 schools.

Governor Whitman's 1997–98 budget proposes a $50-million bond issue to promote and finance extensive networking among the state's institutions of higher education. The bond issue will provide matching funds to colleges and universities that provide a long-range technological plan that will "enhance inter institutional or intrainstitutional connectivity and information technology as it relates to advancing the instructional, research, and service missions of the institution." One likely candidate for bond funds is Rutgers, the state university, which is planning a mega-center in New Brunswick that will connect its distance learning/ITV facilities with up to sixteen remote high school sites.

Another development that may make the statewide cybercampus possible is that, under the recent Telecommunications Act, Bell Atlantic will be able to offer fiber optic connections between local area telephone access (LATA) in north Jersey and LATAs in south Jersey. Until now, federal regulations prevented Bell Atlantic from providing such long-distance service. The new law effectively wipes out LATAs, each one now designated by an area code. Bell Atlantic, for example, can wire colleges and schools in south Jersey so they can receive signals from colleges and schools in north Jersey, and vice versa. The current Bell Atlantic monthly rate for connecting a school via fiber optics is $753.

New Jersey's race toward a cybercampus would seem at first to be at odds with a recent report by the Educational Testing Service (ETS) in Princeton that ranked the state's public school districts below most other states with regard to student-computer ratio and teacher training in computer technology. According to ETS, New Jersey placed 42nd among the states in number of students per multimedia computer (37.5 compared to a national average of 23.7) and ranked 37th in percentage of teachers with at least nine hours of technology training (11 percent compared to a national average of 15 percent).

However, the state's technology establishment advances the following rebuttal:

- ETS student-computer data reflect the 1995–96 school year, when the state was just beginning major strides toward its cybercampus.
- Distance learning and ITV allow large numbers of students to learn at the same time using a very few TV monitors or computer screens. For example, Bergen County College in north Jersey involved 100 middle school students at three locations in a mock constitutional convention.

Bell Atlantic linked approximately 300 high school students at eight sites in Bergen County for a special program called "Celebrating the Vision."
- Since 1995, many more schools in New Jersey have been wired for technology, including access to the Internet.
- New Jersey Intercampus Network (NJIN), created to oversee a technology revolution in higher education, adopted a strategic plan that calls for training at least a third of all college faculty, schoolteachers, and librarians to effectively use new instructional technologies by 2001.

The strategic plan also recommends a "stable funding strategy" to finance "coordinated technology applications for New Jersey's higher education, schools, and library communities." A new education network should be created to provide oversight, planners suggest.

NJIN now guides technology application in higher education, and the Office of Technology in the state Department of Education supervises developments among New Jersey schools. Colleges and universities pay annual dues to NJIN ranging from $2,000 to $5,000. The income helps to support NJIN operations based at Rutgers and at Stevens Institute of Technology.

According to NJIN Executive Director George A. Carroll, the organization fosters networking, shares information (including a Distance Learning Clearinghouse), and seeks grants from the state and other governmental and private sources. The state Office of Technology performs similar functions for schools.

The Distance Learning Clearinghouse consists of college faculty members concerned about training faculty to use the technology. "Many faculty members don't understand technology very well," said George McCloud, Clearinghouse Chairperson, "and some of those who are knowledgeable are ambivalent about it." The clearinghouse will develop teaching protocols for distance learning to prevent professors from "reinventing the wheel," he added. Master schedules also can be compiled to control distance-learning "traffic" between colleges and between colleges and schools.

While much of New Jersey's cybercampus still resides on planning boards and in fertile minds, major projects are underway throughout the state. Two years ago, New Jersey Institute of Technology in Newark and Burlington County College (BCC) in south Jersey together created the Technology and Engineering Center in Mt. Laurel, 15 miles east of Philadelphia, Pennsylvania. TEC, as the three-story brick facility is called, is equipped with three distance-learning classrooms. Professors in Newark and Mount Laurel teach classes at both campuses simultaneously. The TEC classrooms can be linked to seven south Jersey high schools.

TEC also offers students these options:

- Videotapes of classroom instruction that students watch at home.
- Three means of electronic conferencing the professors: e-mail, home page, and via computer directly into the classroom.

Through TEC, students in south Jersey can earn BS degrees from NJIT in computer science, electrical engineering, engineering science, information systems, and engineering technology. TEC also offers a BS degree in science, technology, and society.

In addition to the undergraduate degrees, TEC awards master's degrees in computer science, information systems, and engineering management. Students can earn graduate certificates in managing human resources, programming, telecommunications, and project management. This fall, south Jersey business persons may enroll in a 90-hour, non-credit program on creating Web pages and managing on-site Internet and intranet.

A promising new venture will soon link TEC with seven other colleges and universities in south Jersey to create a regional economic development hub. "The hub will serve academe," said TEC Dean Phillip A. Laplante, "but primarily it will enable small businesses to have access to the Internet and teleconferencing, and their employees can receive training."

NJIT in Newark is participating this fall in a distance learning project sponsored by the World Bank. A videotape of Dr. Rose Dios teaching her calculus course at NJIT will be sent to universities in six African nations: Ethiopia, Ghana, Kenya, Tanzania, Uganda, and Zimbabwe. Students there will see the videotape and then ask questions of Dr. Dios via telephone-satellite hookup.

Networking that the governor's budget might fund on a grand scale is already happening on a small scale. In addition to the arrangement between NJIT and BCC, Rutgers professors are teaching some classes simultaneously to students on the Newark campus of Rutgers and to students at Sussex County College in the northwest corner of the state. Aviation courses originating at Mercer County Technical School are also taken by students at other sites.

M. Robert Hillenbrand, Coordinator of Instructional Services for Bergen County Technical Schools, is one of the pioneers in distance learning and ITV. Using the satellite on the roof of the building in Hackensack, his school already can, theoretically and technically, link 167 schools and colleges, although he has not yet attempted such a feat.

However, during the school year, Bergen Tech routinely connects students at two, three, or four sites for a teleconference on advanced placement physics, U.S. history, and dozens of other subjects. Or he may arrange for remote ITV training for teachers at schools in another county.

"Distance learning and ITV will never replace the live classroom," predicts Phillip Laplante, Dean of TEC in Mt. Laurel, "but tomorrow's college campuses may be smaller, with fewer classroom buildings and dorms."

The cybercampus is not a replacement for the traditional campus in New Jersey, agreed William Reynolds of NJIT, "but an enrichment of traditional campus learning." For example, he said, three high schools or county colleges might like to offer Japanese language instruction, but individually they can't afford a teacher for the small number of students who might enroll in the course at each campus. With distance learning, they *can* afford one teacher for three or six campuses.

Still mostly in the dream stage is the New Jersey Center for Multimedia Research established at NJIT and Princeton University by the State Commission on Science and Technology. The center envisions laboratory experiments and research being shared on a wide scale among colleges and schools throughout the state via distance learning and ITV.

H A N D S O N

1. Consider how you might pursue a part-time career as a freelance writer. Would you become a specialist? If so, in what area(s)? What do you see as the advantages and disadvantages of specialization v. generalization. Reread Emily Willingham's letter.

    - Start an article idea file. This file, unlike the notebook suggested in Chapter Three, should include actual materials collected, such as newspaper and magazine articles and Internet printouts.

    - What space and equipment would you need to establish yourself as a serious freelance writer?

2. Log on to http://www.writersweekly.com/ and scroll through the list of freelance opportunities.

    - Browse a sampling of consumer and trade publications and discover how many articles are written by freelance writers. They may be identified in the masthead in the front of the magazine, at the end of articles, or following their byline ("special correspondent" or words to that effect).

    - Ask your teacher if he/she knows of any current or former students who are working part-time as freelancers. If your teacher can supply a mailing address, e-mail address or phone number, you might want to talk to one or two of these persons to learn how they work.

11 Joining a Magazine's Staff

If there is anything certain about the magazine industry it is this: It can change as fast as the weather when you're counting on a string of perfect vacation days.

Some magazine categories have mushroomed quickly (for example, computer technology) while others have faded (for example, general interest). One year a magazine's backers may feel confident about the niche they have established and the next year close down their pride and joy when they can't find enough subscribers or advertisers, or both. Furthermore, the industry has been inundated nearly overnight (or so it seems) with online versions of print publications and e-zines of every conceivable stripe.

In July 2000, *Folio: the Magazine for Magazine Management* asked four editors to explain how their roles and responsibilities have changed in recent years. This is, in part, what they had to say:

- "Oh, what a difference six years makes! When I became editor in chief of *Family Circle* in 1994, American women had yet to embrace computers, the Internet or cell phones. Our readers wrote letters, not e-mail; they talked about their PTO, not their IPO. My publishing world of the 'Seven Sisters' (*Family Circle, McCall's, Woman's Day, Ladies' Home Journal, Good Housekeeping, Redbook* and *Better Homes and Gardens*) had few competitors. Today, there are lots of what we call 'little sisters vying for our readers. . . ." Susan Ungaro, *Family Circle.*

- "No question, I am expected to be far more Web-savvy than I was even two years ago. Now I'm not just thinking about how a story works in print, but how we do enhanced, expanded versions on our site. More and more frequently I'm asked the simple question: What is your Web strategy? I'm also spending more time editing content that will appear exclusively online. . . ." Geoffrey Brewer, *Sales & Marketing Management.*

- "A sea change swept the publishing industry, along with a raging recession, in the early nineties. It brought the concept of the magazine editor as celebrity. Now, in addition to the normal editor-in-chief stuff, I am also the primary spokesperson for my magazine—the 'face' of the magazine—to trade media, the advertising community and the general news media. Now there are as many presentations to give as manuscripts to edit, as many marketing campaigns to nurture as vouchers to sign." Joe Oldham, *Popular Mechanics.*

- "There are more magazines today than there have ever been, which makes the competition even fiercer. And since this is a world that is easily excited by the new, and often bored by the old, it has become more challenging than ever to run a magazine that has a tradition and a history. Since I am editor in chief of one magazine that has been around for more than a century, as well as a vigorous startup, I know that editors of magazines new or old worry about the same things." Myrna Blyth, *Ladies' Home Journal* and *More.*

Here are two general observations about magazine staffs:

- It is not uncommon for writers and editors to move from one magazine to another, most frequently within the same genre or specialization (e.g., from *TWA Ambassador* to *Sky,* both inflight magazines). Ms. Blyth of *Ladies' Home Journal* said she has been editor in chief for 20 years. She is decidedly the exception.

- While Ms. Blyth is an exception when it comes to longevity, she is typical in another way: Females are filling more editorial positions than ever before—and not just among so-called women's magazines. For example, of the 26 editorial staff positions on tradition-bound *Yankee Magazine* in Spring 2000, nearly two-thirds were filled by females. Among the first four national business and finance publications listed in *Writer's Market 2000,* a woman is listed as editor, co-editor or managing editor for three of them.

Getting Started

Typical entry level position titles on a magazine are editorial secretary, editorial assistant, production assistant, and researcher. On some publications, the roles and responsibilities of editorial secretary and editorial assistant may be similar, but ordinarily the editorial secretary, as the title implies, is responsible for performing secretarial or general office functions. One publication advertising for the position stated that the person hired would be "expected to do whatever is needed to aid the editors in gathering information to publish."

The typical editorial assistant is given some opportunities to write. For example, the same publication that was looking for an editorial secretary also was hiring an editorial assistant and listed as one of the primary duties:

"Compiles, writes, and edits on-going sections, such as calendar and new products." The editorial assistant also may be the first person to evaluate queries from freelancers, deciding which ones are worth submitting to an editor for final determination. In addition, she (more often than he) may be asked to perform initial copy editing of manuscripts sent in by freelance writers.

The production assistant helps those editors responsible for final copy editing, page layout and design, and printing. This person in particular, but almost anyone seeking a position on a magazine's staff (and expecting to move up the staff ladder), should know basic page layout and design using Quark XPress or other comparable program. Lee Beadling, who landed a position as staff writer for *Orthopedics Today* right after graduating from college, said one of the reasons he was hired as a staff writer rather than editorial assistant was because of his knowledge of Quark Xpress, learned as a reporter/editor for his college's newspaper.

All editors on all publications expect articles to be thoroughly and reliably researched. Therefore, the position of researcher on a magazine's staff is an important one. The researcher primarily serves staff writers and editors who need assistance in finding source material or checking facts. However, the researcher also may go over manuscripts submitted by freelance writers to ensure their accuracy.

Becoming a Staff Writer

What surprises teachers of magazine article writing is the number of students who profess an interest in working for a magazine after graduation but who have no interest in or time for the college's newspaper or magazine. The second and more important reason why he was hired as a staff writer rather than editorial assistant, Beadling said, is because he had a lot of clippings of articles he had written for the college newspaper. "Get clips," is the terse advice from Marie Rosenthal, editor in chief of the internal medicine group of publications at Slack Inc., the publishing company that hired Beadling. The clippings can be from college publications or from local weekly and daily newspapers.

Regardless of the publication—trade or consumer, print or online, highbrow or lowbrow—and regardless of the magazine genre—religion, men's fitness, insurance, etc.—editors hire men and women who are competent writers. Editors will train their writers to become knowledgeable in the magazine's specialization or niche. Remember, Beadling had not a clue about orthopedics surgery when he went to work for *Orthopedics Today.* But he knew how to write; he already was a proven, capable journalist. He learned about orthopedics surgery on the job—and later became something of an authority on the subject.

A staff writer's responsibility is pretty clear: he or she writes primarily feature articles for the magazine. The staff writer also may write shorter pieces for special sections of the magazine. "I wrote all day every day," Beadling said about his time as a staff writer. Of course, when a person says he writes articles, you understand by now that he is talking about all the steps in the writing process, including and foremost careful research. In Beadling's case, for example, writing also meant attending medical conventions and hearings before the Federal Drug Administration, and phone calls to sources around the world.

It is important to note that persons with the title of staff writer may not be the only persons on staff who write articles. Also, some magazines employ no staff writers and depend almost totally on freelancers and/or news releases. Editorial assistants may be given some writing responsibilities. In addition, persons with the title of senior editor, assistant editor, or editor of a special section (e.g., news briefs, fashion, dining out, and so on) may write feature articles, opinion pieces or other, shorter items. The mastheads of some magazines list senior writers as well as staff writers. The distinction between the two usually is based on proven ability as a journalist, familiarity with the magazine's specialty or niche, and experience (length of service).

Freelance writers looking through a guidebook such as *Writer's Market* search for those publications that report they are 75% to 100% freelance written. This is their kind of magazine, but it probably is not the best choice for someone wanting a position as staff writer. However, while a magazine may depend on freelance writers for the bulk of its content, it may hire a staff writer to be responsible for each issue's primary feature article. For example, a magazine's listing in *Writer's Market* may state that article length varies from 200 to 2,000 words. The magazine may want freelance writers to contribute shorter pieces—say 200–750 words—while each issue's single long feature of 2,000 words is reserved for the magazine's staff writer. As a rule, however, if you are interested in becoming a staff writer, go after those publications that depend mostly or exclusively on staff writers.

Typically, the qualifications for entry level positions and staff writers include a bachelor's degree, preferably with a major in journalism or communication, and competency in Microsoft Word or equivalent computer program. Prior experience on a college or professional publication is a plus.

Moving Up

Since many magazine staffs consist of only three or four persons, moving up may mean moving out to a larger publication. If the editor in chief is the next step up from staff writer and the editor in chief is happy and reasonably successful in the position, then upward mobility on that publication doesn't exist.

On the other hand, the staff of larger publications may offer a wide variety of opportunities for movement. Take, for example, *Seventeen* magazine. The masthead of *Seventeen* lists 20 editorial positions above editorial assistant and staff writer. These include editors and associate editors serving various sections of the magazine: fashion, beauty, entertainment, departments (e.g., "Your Room" and "School Zone") and features (major articles that do not fit into the other categories). Also included are copy chief, associate copy editor, copy editor, and research chief.

Particularly noteworthy, considering the major changes occurring in the industry, is a staff listing for the magazine's online version: www.seventeen.com. The web site is under the direction of an online editor, associate online editor, online community coordinator (presumably in charge of responding to feedback from online readers), and assistant online editor.

Many publications, when they first go online, try to curtail expenses by using the existing print staff for the online version. At the start, the online content is often simply a scaled down sampling of what the print magazine is offering. As the online publication takes on a life of its own, however, the content, including some feature articles, may be entirely different from the print publication. Also, as the *Seventeen* masthead illustrates, online publications often emphasize reader involvement more than print versions. Therefore, be alert to the possibility of moving from one version of a magazine to the other—and maybe back again.

Pleasing Advertisers

Depending on the nature of a publication and its policy, editors and writers for both consumer and trade periodicals may be influenced in selection of subject matter and article slant or angle by advertisers (or at least by the magazine's advertising staff). This is particularly true among magazines whose departments or sections roughly correspond to the kinds of advertisements solicited. For example, if a health and fitness magazine's advertising staff is selling a lot of space to companies that manufacture, sell, or distribute products designed to improve nutrition or enhance lifestyle, chances are very good that the editorial staff will be expected to write articles that encourage readers to use those kinds of products, even if particular manufacturers or brand names are not mentioned.

The relationship between advertising and editorial content is especially close on some women's magazines, where articles in such departments as beauty and fashion often mirror messages contained in ads featured on the same or nearby pages. Gloria Steinem addressed the issue in the premier edition of *Ms. Magazine* in 1990: "There [in women's magazines] it isn't just a little content that's devoted to attracting ads, it's almost all of it. If *Time* and

Newsweek had to lavish praise on cars in general and credit General Motors in particular to get GM ads, there would be a scandal—maybe a criminal investigation. When women's magazines from *Seventeen* to *Lears* [now out of print] praise beauty products in general and credit Revlon in particular to get ads, it's just business as usual."

FOR EXAMPLE

Folio: the Magazine for Magazine Management conducts an annual editorial salary survey of consumer and trade publications. The results of the 2000 survey were first published on pages 37 to 42 in the August 2000 issue of the publication. The article reporting the survey results and several of the accompanying charts follow (see Figure 11.1).

> *"Managing Editors See Huge Gains"*
> **By Bob Moseley**
> **(Reprinted by permission of Folio: the Magazine for Magazine Management)**
> Was it a good year to be an editor? That depends on your particular job title, according to the results of Folio's 2000 Editorial Salary Survey. While pay for managing editors skyrocketed an average 18.8 percent and the top editorial position, editorial director/editor in chief, showed a healthy 8.2 percent gain, compensation for executive editors was flat. Pay for senior editors rose dramatically on the b-to-b side [business-to-business, or trade publications], but modestly for those at consumer magazines.
>
> Managing editor may be the position most in demand, judging from the enormous 23.2 percent leap in business [trade] salaries and 15.7 percent growth on the consumer side. For the second time in three years, there was double-digit growth in both trade and consumer pay, resulting in an average salary of $57,125. Managing editors on the trade side continue to narrow the gap between themselves and their consumer counterparts, with an average base salary of $55,492, compared to $58,592 for those at consumer titles.
>
> Competition from dot.coms may be one reason for the robust salary increases, according to Tom Nawrocki, managing editor at *George* [now defunct]. "There are a lot more places to lose people to," he says. "I think that's been a help. On the Internet, you need a managing editor to do most of the work because assignments are small in scope."
>
> Compensation for editorial directors/editors in chief continues to grow at a brisk pace, on the heels of a 9.1 percent increase in 1999. The average salary for editorial director is $93,329, thanks to compound growth of 7.5 percent over five years. Again, b-to-b growth is outpacing consumer, but the gap between average salaries is narrowing—$94,067 for consumer and $92,727 for business.
>
> It may be that editors in chief are being compensated for taking on extra responsibilities. "I'm doing 90 percent of the editor in chief position, while that person works primarily on the Web site and launches," says one managing editor.

2000 Editorial Salary Survey

Editorial Dossier

Men dominate at the top jobs, while the managing editor role is filled mainly by women. The Northeast, especially New York City, is still the most lucrative place to work.

MEN **OUTEARN** WOMEN

The largest pay disparity is at the editorial director/editor in chief level, with males, who dominate the field, earning 18 percent higher salaries, on average. The only position where pay is equitable is editor/executive editor—where the division of jobs between men and women is more equally split.

AVERAGE

EDITORIAL DIRECTOR/EDITOR IN CHIEF	
Male	$99,030
Female	$84,276

EDITOR/EXECUTIVE EDITOR	
Male	$64,994
Female	$64,225

MANAGING EDITOR	
Male	$61,089
Female	$54,039

SENIOR EDITOR	
Male	$64,247
Female	$55,757

AVERAGE SALARIES
BY REGION

New York City and the Northeast continue to pay the highest editorial salaries, with the heartland of America—the North Central zone—paying the least. The difference is particularly pronounced at the editorial director level, where those in New York City earn more than $35,000 over their North Central counterparts.

	EDITORIAL DIRECTOR/ EDITOR IN CHIEF	EDITOR/ EXECUTIVE EDITOR	MANAGING EDITOR	SENIOR EDITOR
New York City	$113,216	$80,828	$70,204	$70,612
Northeast	$107,940	$74,628	$63,565	$67,406
South	$84,473	$64,698	$59,587	*
North Central	$77,804	$56,556	$52,203	$50,130
West	$103,206	*	*	*

* NOT ENOUGH INFORMATION SUPPLIED TO REPORT RESULTS

THE DIVISION
OF LABOR

BIGGER COMPANY,
LARGER SALARY

Not only do the larger companies pay more—sometimes as much as $18,000 more for the same job title—the disparity between salaries for men and women is not always quite as marked.

	LESS THAN $15 MILLION IN ANNUAL REVENUE	$15 MILLION OR MORE IN ANNUAL REVENUE
Editorial director/ Editor in chief		
Male	$88,049	$107,038
Female	$72,537	$105,192
Editor/Executive editor		
Male	$56,620	$74,795
Female	$55,835	$75,714
Managing editor		
Male	*	$64,212
Female	$50,803	$59,773
Senior editor		
Male	*	$69,062
Female	$49,585	$60,312

* NOT ENOUGH INFORMATION SUPPLIED TO REPORT RESULTS

EDITORIAL DIRECTOR/EDITOR IN CHIEF
FEMALE 40% MALE 60%

EDITOR OR EXECUTIVE EDITOR
FEMALE 47% MALE 53%

MANAGING EDITOR
FEMALE 59% MALE 41%

SENIOR EDITOR
FEMALE 47% MALE 53%

FIGURE 11.1

First published in *Folio: The Magazine for Magazine Management*, August, 2000. Used with permission.

Although the top editorial position is showing healthy gains, just one step down the pay has been flat. Editors/executive editors saw minuscule 0.1 percent growth—part of a three-year trend of smaller raises—with b-to-b salaries dropping slightly after a 7.4 percent increase last year. Executive editors on the consumer side still earn appreciably more ($68,367) than trade editors ($60,904).

Senior editors' compensation rose 10 percent, to an average base salary of $60,166. But that increase was buoyed by the b-to-b side, where a 17.9 percent increase was nearly six times that of the consumer increase (2.9 percent). Here again, trade magazines ($56,368) are closing the salary gap with consumer books ($63,363).

Other findings from the survey:

- Men are outearning women by substantial amounts, except at the editor/executive editor level, where they are almost even ($64,994 for men, $64,225 women). The gulf is widest at editorial director ($99,030 for men, $84,276 women).
- Male editorial directors/editors-in-chief who are 40 or older average $15,000 more ($100,733) than women in the same position who are 40 or older ($85,178). The difference is also startling for male senior editors 40 and older ($70,426) compared to female senior editors 40 and older ($55,560).
- Generally, editors with less than five years of experience make substantially more at consumer titles than at b-to-b magazines.

Stacey Herriott took a college course in magazine article writing in Fall 1994 and graduated the next Spring. Five months later she started freelancing for *Casino Journal*, the trade publication for the casino industry in America, which has offices in Las Vegas and Atlantic City (Herriott lived near Atlantic City). Its 1999 circulation among casino executives, managers, and others in the business was 25,000.

By December 1995, Herriott was a part-time staff writer for *Casino Journal*. Early in 1996 she went full time as an assistant editor. As of Summer 2000, Herriott was an associate editor for *Casino Player*, a monthly consumer magazine based in Atlantic City with a circulation of 200,000; she also was associate editor of *Strictly Slots*, a more recent publication of Ace Marketing Inc. Says Herriott, "For Strictly Slots, I interview and write about big casino winners—how their winning affected their lives." While most of her time is spent in Atlantic City, she has traveled to casinos elsewhere. For example, Herriott attended the opening of Atlantis, Paradise Island, in The Bahamas and has written about casino operations along the Gulf of Mexico in Mississippi.

"When I began freelancing for *Casino Journal*, the only thing I knew about casinos was that they had slot machines and buffets. Period. I've learned a lot since then." As if being associate editor of two major magazines is not enough, Herriott also edits a newsletter titled *Atlantic City Insider* and serves as a vice president of the Atlantic City Junior Chamber of Commerce.

What follows is Herriott's article about Atlantis, Paradise Island, that appeared in the May 2000 issue of *Casino Player.*

"Betting on the Beach"
by Stacey Herriott
Many people—and you can count me among them—will tell you Atlantis, Paradise Island in The Bahamas is one of the most amazing places on earth.

Cascading waterfalls. Fish and other sea life at every turn. Eleven million gallons of water for aquatic activities and attractions. Stunning architecture. Miles of sandy white beaches with blue crystalline waters.

But what many people don't know is this premier vacation destination offers a beautiful casino with competitive slot payback percentages, the newest gaming machines and plenty of table action. If you haven't visited Paradise Island since it was owned and operated by Merv Griffin's Resorts International, then you have never really been to Paradise Island.

Sun International bought Paradise Island in 1994 for $125 million. The property, which was rundown at the time of purchase, included Paradise Island Resort & Casino, the Ocean Golf & Tennis Club and Paradise Island. Sun's chairman, Sol Kerzner, had a vision to transform the resort complex into a major destination in The Bahamas.

Since acquiring the property, Sun International has invested more than $850-million in the casino-resort to create a must-see attraction in the Caribbean. Atlantis emerged from Paradise Island like a temple rising out of the sea several years later. It creates a window into the mythical past of the Lost Continent of Atlantis; its theme is incomparable to any gaming property in the United States.

When Sun International unveiled the $600-million Royal Towers in December of 1998, Atlantis became the largest family entertainment and gaming island resort in the world. Since then, the oasis has attracted high rollers with million-dollar credit lines and celebrities ranging from the king of shock-talk radio, Howard Stern, to movie star Kevin Costner.

It's no wonder Atlantis attracts such an elite crowd of guests. In fact, it's evident the moment you step into the Royal Towers' Great Hall of Waters lobby. Etched into the 70-foot ceiling dome are a cluster of golden seashells. Neomosaic style murals positioned throughout the lobby retell the story of the ancient island of Atlantis and its impending doom. Black, gold, cream and deep orange tones add to the elegance. Wrought iron light fixtures with fire-orange scones decorate the walls.

The Café at the Great Hall of Waters descends several stairs from the lobby entrance. The underwater ruins of Atlantis surround guests in this casual, yet sophisticated restaurant. Water cascades in nearby fountains and swift-gliding fish rendezvous around rock and coral inside the tanks. Waiters in long white aprons serve Continental cuisine with an American twist.

Like the entire resort, the attention to detail in the lobby is spectacular. But that's no surprise, either. Kerzner, who is legendary for hands-on supervision of every aspect of his resorts, played an integral role in the creation of Atlantis. Not only did he oversee the resort's design concept, he even assisted with choosing the colors for the guest rooms. He also commissioned renowned artists, whose works have appeared in major museums, the White House and in prestigious private collections, to create artwork for the Royal Towers.

The Royal Towers are the setting for more than 1,200 guest rooms situated in two towers. Accommodations are available in a variety of categories, including queen and king rooms, as well as the Imperial Club's junior, executive and grand suites. All rooms have five-star quality appointments such as mini bars, in-room safes, hair dryers, irons and French balconies with water views.

Some of the greatest views are from inside the Bridge Suite, which is perched high on a bridge connecting the towers. The suite, reserved for $1 million-players like basketball great Michael Jordan, boasts panoramic views of the ocean, nearby Nassau and the property's Marina from its ceiling-to-floor windows. Daytime talk show host Oprah Winfrey has also been known to call the Bridge Suite home while vacationing in The Bahamas.

The door of the 10-room suite swings open to a grand foyer with Italian marble flooring and 12-foot high ceilings. The massive living area exudes a warm ambiance with hues of red, gold and black. Designer furnishings and glass tables sit atop hand-tufted rugs. A baby grand piano and two entertainment centers are just a few of the opulent amenities.

When it's play time, a lounge area doubles as a gaming and entertainment center with a marble inlaid chessboard and a full-service bar. Next to the kitchen is a dining room highlighted by a wrought iron and 22-karat gold chandelier, which hovers above a 10-seat table with gilt armchairs.

The suite's king bedroom includes a sitting area, his and her baths and closets, a desk and an entertainment armoire. Velvet pillows, hand-painted linens and a custom coverlet adorn a four-poster bed. The bath area's amenities include chaise lounge chairs, picture windows, and marble showers complete with bath fixtures that resemble dolphins.

The queen bedroom is equally as elegant.

In addition to the Royal Towers, there's the Coral and Beach Towers with 1,126 rooms. They feature two queen beds or one king-sized bed, television, hair dryers, irons and a balcony. The motif integrates tropical colors and textures with Caribbean-style furniture and art. Aquatic-themed bedspreads in coral hues mix well with the warm sea green and soft turquoise accents.

The Atlantis entertainment complex links the three towers together with more than 100,000 sq. ft. of gaming, entertainment and dining space. The casino floor occupies a majority of the area with its 980 slot machines and 78 table games.

Sunlight pours into the casino through numerous skylights and windows, providing a front row seat to the property's waterscape. It emanates a colorful energy with brilliant glass sculptures by artist Dale Chihuly, who is also known for his work at Bellagio in Las Vegas. The "Temple of The Sun" looks like an enormous ball of fiery red and orange flames set atop a carved block of stone. The creation is animated by illuminated murals of lightning bolts, the sun and fire.

Chihuly also designed another focal point in the casino, the "Temple of the Moon." The massive blue crystal ball with white accents is the highlight of the casino's information center. Gold and blue paintings of mythical characters dance around the sculpture.

Above the table games are faux octopi clinging to light fixtures, which hang from the mouths of dolphin ornaments.

The casino has a blend of table games including blackjack, craps, roulette, mini baccarat, and Caribbean Stud Poker. Table limits range from $15 to $5,000. The casino also hosts a variety of high-end table game tournaments throughout the year, which often feature $1 million prize packages.

In comparison to most island resort casinos, Atlantis offers slot players a mix of the newest games, such as Williams' Jackpot Party and Reel 'Em In. Players will also find old-time favorites like Red, White and Blue, Double Diamonds and Bally GameMakers. Not only are the machine selections good, but wide aisles and spacious machine placement make playing slots here a pleasant experience. Denominations range from 25-cents to $100.

With seven $100 slots and some high-stake table games, the casino attracts its share of premium players. What many don't know is there's gaming value for every type of player. There's plenty of quarter machines and $1 games that reign king here. The casino will also have nickel games up-and-running in late Spring.

The biggest myth centering around Atlantis has nothing to do with the lost continent. It's the misconception that the casino's slot payback percentages are extremely low. In reality, the numbers are rather competitive. As proof, the casino awarded more than $452 million in slot payouts last year. Also, the U.S. dollar is on par with the Bahamian dollar, and all machines are equipped with bill validators to accept American currency.

One of the greatest differences between Atlantis and casinos in the U.S. is jackpots are paid as fast as the power boats that speed by the marina. Unlike other gaming jurisdictions, there's less paperwork to record. Once a player signs on the dotted line (this verifies the winning combination), they receive their loot without annoying delays.

Another convenience for players is the resort's room key cards that double as rate cards. There's no cashback program, but loyal players are rewarded through comps. Also, the casino features a "Lucky Star" program, which randomly awards "stars" at every slot. The stars act as entries into a bi-weekly drawing, held every Wednesday and Saturday. It awards $1,000 in cash prizes, including $500 to the big winner. Players can find out how many lucky stars they have accumulated by visiting the "Temple of the Sun."

A diverse offering of dining and entertainment venues encircles the gaming environment. Dragons nightclub hosts some of the island's hottest bands and its in-house DJ, "Joey Jam," has a long career of spinning tunes for celebrities. The place is hopping both day and night. Glass windows encase the club, providing an ocean view if you can look past the bar's 15-foot sea dragon.

Players who have a rating at another casino are encouraged to call the casino marketing department prior to visiting Atlantis. Some research will determine if you qualify for a casino hotel rate.

Casino action is only a part of the resort's appeal. The marine life at the resort more than doubled in size when the Royal Towers opened. As a result,

Atlantis became the world's largest tropical marine habitat—second only to mother nature. The resort also put a unique spin on the notion of water rides.

More than 50,000 sea animals—200 species of marine life—live among the waters of Atlantis. In the crystal clear waters, fish clamber about waiting for the next feeding. A staff of 60 expert seakeepers care for the guests living in the underwater passages that zigzag around the property. Schools of fish dart in and out of small rocky crevices in several of the 11 exhibit lagoons. A 100-foot underwater pedestrian walkway and a suspension rope bridge is the ticket to a parade of giant sharks, sawfish and other interesting marine creatures.

Sea critters are also an integral part of The Dig, a depiction of the archaeological rediscovery of Atlantis. Walk-by tanks and interactive displays take visitors on an undersea journey through a cave-like maze of passageways and tunnels. A line of sharks and a colorful array of tropical fish follow stingrays as they flutter their sea wings. Underwater vistas spill out into boulevards and streets, which display the ruins of Atlantis. The cavernous hallways showcase the laboratories of ancient Atlanteans along with their inventions of electricity, flying machines and submarines.

Around every corner are tanks of ocean animals, including iridescent jellyfish and squirming eels. More than 700 poisonous Indian Ocean Lionfish patrol the waters, while 400 piranha guard the Royal Treasury of Ancient Atlantis. Don't miss Earle, a 300-pound grouper, who is expected to weigh-in at 1,000 pounds one day.

The aquatic adventure continues outside The Dig with numerous water rides. Slippery slides provide adrenaline rushes for thrill seekers, and pools of various depths and configurations accommodate those looking for a quieter bit of fun.

A life-size replica of an ancient Mayan Temple, surrounded by jungle foliage, is the water park's main attraction. The temple houses several water slides, including the "Leap of Faith." This daring slide propels riders down a 60-ft., almost-vertical drop at tremendous speed. The ride lasts less than 30 seconds and comes to an end as riders dash through a clear acrylic tunnel submerged in a shark-filled lagoon.

The Serpent slide, 48 ft. up the temple, spins riders into a winding trail of darkness before they emerge in a Predator Lagoon to view sharks. The temple also features "The Challenge," two high-speed dueling slides, and "The Jungle Slide," which meanders through jungles and caves. Several other slides offer youngsters gentle trips.

Along with twisting and spiraling water slides, there are more than 10 different swimming areas to choose from. Options include tubing down a lazy river and peering at tropical fish while snorkeling in a seven-acre saltwater lagoon.

As with any resort of this magnitude, there are dining options to appeal to a variety of culinary desires. The smorgasbord of choices run the gamut from poolside sandwiches to the Asian specialities of Mama Loo's. With an inventory of 38 restaurants, bars and lounges, choosing a place to eat isn't always easy.

The most elegant and romantic restaurant is Fathoms. It offers a menu of fresh seafood from around the world in addition to a raw bar. Tiger prawns, calamari, lobster, shrimp, scallops and a tempting assortment of oysters are just a few of the possibilities. The food is just as amazing as the setting. The dimly lit dining area is accented by ancient murals and windows that reveal sharks swarming around fish and rainbow-colored coral formations. Bright mosaic tiles pave the way to plank wood tables. New age music accompanies the fare.

Another dining gem is Five Twins, located directly off the casino floor. Inspired by the famous 18th century artist Piranesi, the restaurant has Roman character. A massive 20-foot iron gate spills out onto stone floors, mosaics and elegant tones of ivory, gold and silver. Guests can also dine on a terrace featuring views of the marina and Bahamian sunsets. Five Twins, named for the sons of Poseidon, serves Pacific Rim cuisine with a fusion of Asian spices and seafood specialities. It also has a cigar bar stocked with the finest Cuban cigars and vintage rums.

The nautical setting of Voyagers makes it a cozy breakfast nook with sweeping views of the casino and the ocean. An oversized ship hangs from the ceiling, along with a map of the ancient world that showcases Atlantean travels. The look is topped off with a 12-foot chandelier designed to resemble a compass. The eatery specializes in New York-style bagels, pastries and gourmet coffee.

Atlas Grille and Bar is another example of casual dining at resort. It's similar to a Planet Hollywood, minus all the movie memorabilia. The restaurant is in the shape of a Roman chariot track with a bar in the center. Above the tables are illuminated spheres of multi-colored glass. The menu of American fare features burgers, oversized sandwiches and root beer floats.

Naturally, there is no shortage of fast food outlets scattered throughout the resort. One of the best kept secrets is the Clock Tower, housed on an outdoor terrace overlooking the marina. Boats and million-dollar yachts glide across calm waters as waiters serve oven-baked pizza, beer and strawberry daiquiris.

Food is far from cheap at Atlantis, so inquire about the resort's cost-saving dining plans. Additionally, the food outlets automatically include a 15-percent gratuity on all food and beverage tabs.

An afternoon snack in a chaise lounge by the pool may be relaxing, but nothing compares to what happens when you walk inside The Spa at Atlantis. The aroma of lush tropical plants and the soothing sounds of water running over rocks create a tranquil atmosphere inside the 25,000-square foot facility. Through blending scientific discoveries with ancient wisdom and ritual, the spa is a retreat from the daily stresses of life. It features 14 private treatments rooms, including two lavish suites for specialty therapies.

While the spa provides a full complement of massage therapies, it also offers facials, seaweed treatments and the Thermal Baths of Utopia (a series of saunas, steams and showers). Among the menu of indulgences is Poseidon's Thalassotherpay Pool. Thousands of gallons of fresh seawater powerfully massage the entire body for 15 minutes to help dissolve muscle pains, increase circulation and speed-up sluggish metabolism. Guests can wrap themselves in a fluffy robe and nap on one of the spa's relaxation chairs once the session is complete.

Treatments cost anywhere from $15 for the Thalassotherpay Pool to $199 for two hours of pampering inside the Queen Cleito Suite.

Tucked away from the treatment rooms is a fitness center featuring state-of-the-art cardiovascular equipment, strength training machines and free weights. A complete program of fitness activities ranging from low impact step aerobics to power yoga round out the offerings.

As a family vacation destination, Atlantis has a never-ending schedule of children's activities. Through the resort's Discovery Channel Camp, kids (ages five to 12) can explore Atlantis' attractions with trained counselors.

Like the Discovery Channel's programming, the camp takes a hands-on approach to educating children about the oceanic world. The fun begins at Base Camp, a replica of the famous Spanish galleon, *Atocha,* that sank in the Bahamian seas in the early 1600s. The play and orientation area has everything from a "Science Outpost," featuring microscopes and touch tanks to a "Technology Lab" with computers.

While there's plenty of indoor activities, the interactive educational program also ensconces youngsters in several outdoor escapades. During the day, campers can join expeditions around Atlantis to learn more about sea life and watch sharks being fed. Other programs include an "Undersea Safari" for snorkeling and animal collecting as well as "It's A Smash," which teaches participants what it's like to be an archaeologist.

Once the children are off discovering the wonders of Atlantis, it's time to break out the shopping bags. There are more than 22 stores scattered throughout the resort, which offer everything from logo merchandise to silk scarves and emerald jewels. However, the centerpiece of shopping at Atlantis is Crystal Court, a collection of designer boutiques, located just a few steps from the casino.

The entrance to the Crystal Court Shops is marked by one of Chihuly's glass sculptures, "Crystal Gate," an 18 foot-high sculpture made out of 3,100 hand-blown crystals. From there, the shiny marble walkway leads to high-end stores such as Gucci, Versace and Cartier. While most of the shops are pricey, there are options for smaller budgets, such as Atlantis Sport International, offering casual wear, and the Atlantis Logo Shop, which sells everything from toys to luggage. More shopping venues are located in the Royal, Coral and Beach Towers.

One of the benefits of a shopping spree in The Bahamas is that purchases are duty-free. This policy allows travelers to take home duty-free purchases up to $600 (providing they have been out of the country for at least 48 hours). Also, in many cases, brand name items are 25 to 35 percent cheaper than in the U.S.

In addition to the many shops within the resort, there's the Bahamian Craft Center on the Paradise Island-end of the eastern-most bridge to Atlantis. The brightly colored dome structure features works from some of the country's most talented artisans. Fine art, wood carvings, clothing, jewelry and specialty foods are among the items for sale.

For those who want to venture off Paradise Island for a shopping excursion, try Downtown Nassau. Clothing boutiques, craft stores, and antique shops line Bay Street. Perhaps the best bargains are found in the straw market area. Local craftsmen showcase their wares and a little haggling usually results in a good deal.

Of course, paying for goods in the islands is never a problem. Most merchants accept either U.S. or Bahamian currency as well as all major American credit cards.

In less than a decade, Sun International has not just created another resort, but a complete destination. With more than 2,300 rooms, a variety of restaurants and lounges, a shopping center, a 24-hour casino, sandy white beaches and dozens of water attractions, visitors will never have a reason to leave Atlantis.

The resort's beauty is coupled with personal attention and hospitality, which makes this a memorable island getaway for everyone. Kerzner set out to create a place for people of all walks of life and succeeded. The guests are a thorough mix of young, old, sedate and active. There's also the people who enjoy the casino and engage in a little bit of nightlife once the sun sets the sky aflame in a palate of mauves, pinks, oranges and violets.

While Atlantis capitalizes on the tropical appeal of the islands, it creates its own scenery through the genius of architects and visionaries like Kerzner, who want to keep the surprises coming. As a result, it's almost impossible to see and experience everything the resort has to offer in just a few days.

However, in the end, you'll leave thinking you've discovered the lost continent—hopefully, with some casino winnings as your reward.

While in college, where he majored in journalism, Matthew Sedita worked as a part-time stringer for both a weekly and a daily newspaper. He also served as film editor for www.hipnosis.com, an e-zine covering entertainment and the arts primarily in New Jersey. The position offered experience but no salary.

A year after graduating from college, he became assistant editor of *J14*, a magazine aimed primarily at girls aged 8–16. On some publications, *J14* included, the position of assistant editor is equivalent to staff writer—a step above the typical entry level position of editorial assistant. Sedita credits his part-time work while in college and the clippings those assignments provided as the reason he skipped over the entry level position.

J14 is a recent addition to the stable of magazines published by the German firm Bauer Publishing Company. Other magazines published by Bauer include *Woman's World, First for Women, Soap Opera Update,* and *Soaps in Depth.*

Here is Sedita's first major article for *J14*, which appeared in the August 2000 edition. It is titled "How Freddie Overcame Heartbreak."

"How Freddie Overcame Heartbreak"
by Matthew Sedita
(Reprinted by permission of **J14** *magazine and Bauer Publishing Company)*
Things were not always as wonderful for Freddie Prinze Jr. as they are today. When his longtime girlfriend, actress Kimberly McCullough, dumped him last winter, Freddie was devastated. He never thought he would get over the pain caused by the end of his four-year relationship. But he's bounced back and is in love again. Recently, the hottie sat down with *J14* and told us how he mended his broken heart—and how you can do the same!

"She bounced," said Freddie about McCullough. "It's not like Kimberly was mean and broke my heart and crushed it. Something that we had that was very special came to an end, and it's heartbreaking."

Well, he's recovered. He also has advice for those of you who might also be going through heartbreak. "You always can bounce back—you just have to allow yourself to do that, and know that there's always somebody out there for you, and if one doesn't work out that you know was the perfect one, guess what? There's going to be someone else that you know is the perfect one, so it's ok."

And bounce back Freddie has. His new love is "Buffy the Vampire Slayer"'s Sarah Michelle Gellar. The two met on the set of "I Know What You Did Last Summer." This time, Freddie is being private about his love life. "I dated Kimberly for four years. We were open about our relationship, which got us a lot of flack. This time, I'm keeping tight-lipped about [Sarah]."

Well, the cat is really out of the bag. Freddie and Sarah were seen smooching at this year's MTV Movie Awards in June. "Nothing feels better than being in love. It's the greatest high in the world, especially if you throw it out there and say, 'This is how I feel,' and you're hoping they feel the same way, and when they do, nothing beats that." It looks like this Prinze has finally found his princess.

Accompanying the main article was the following sidebar under the title "Rumor Mill."

Living in the spotlight, celebrities are often targets of gossip. Some of it's true, but often it's totally made up. See if you can guess which of the following statements are true about Freddie. The answers are in the lower left corner of this page.

1. Freddie will guest star on Sarah's show "Buffy the Vampire Slayer" next season.
2. Freddie is a good cook and loves to cook for Sarah.
3. Freddie desperately wants to play Spider Man in an upcoming film about the superhero.
4. Sarah and Freddie are engaged to be married.
5. Freddie and Sarah started dating when they both starred in "I Know What You Did Last Summer."

"Answers 2 and 3 are true."

HANDS ON

1. Examine the mastheads of a variety of consumer and trade publications, both print and online, to learn about the different editorial staff positions and titles. Determine which are entry level positions and what opportunities might exist for moving up into higher level positions.

   - Check out the employment section in the Sunday edition of a major daily newspaper. What kinds of magazine positions are being advertised and what qualifications or experience are required?

2. If you are not familiar with or competent in Quark XPress, find out if you can learn the system from a course or by working for a college publication.

   • Either as a class activity or on your own interview an editorial assistant, assistant editor, or staff writer for a local, regional, or national publication. Your teacher may suggest someone or arrange for the interview. Learn first hand about the duties and responsibilities of that person.

APPENDIX A

Glossary of Terms

Anecdote   A very short account of a real incident. The story has a beginning, middle, and end.

Angle   One author's approach to a subject. The aspect of a story the author chooses to emphasize or focus on.

Byline   The name of the author of an article.

Clips   Actual clippings or photocopies of articles previously published.

Copyright   Under current copyright law, any manuscript you write is automatically copyrighted, which simply means you have sole, legal right to the manuscript. It is your property. (Also, see Rights.)

Cover Letter   A business letter that accompanies a manuscript submitted to an editor. The letter briefly informs the editor about the manuscript and provides any additional information the editor needs to know.

Department   A special, recurring section of a magazine. For example, letters to the editor would be a department.

E-zine   A Web magazine that caters to very narrow interests. It is not an online version of a print magazine.

Feature   A major article in a publication, usually longer than material included in the publication's various departments. (See Department.)

Formula   The lineup of departments and sections in a magazine that is the same from one issue to the next, recognized in the magazine's table of contents.

Kill Fee   Payment to an author for time and effort expended completing an assignment when the magazine has decided against accepting the article for publication. (See also Payments to Author.)

Lead   The opening paragraph of a query letter or article.

Masthead   A list of a magazine's editorial and advertising staff members, usually located on one of the first half dozen pages of a magazine.

Niche   A narrow focus of content and audience within a larger area of specialization. For example, *Skydiving* magazine fills a niche in the sports specialization. (See also Specialization.)

Online Magazine   While some magazines are found strictly on the Internet (e.g., *Salon*), in most cases an online magazine is the Internet version of a print magazine.

Payments to Author Magazines pay authors for their work in one of two ways: "on acceptance" or "on publication". "On acceptance" means the author will be paid within three to five weeks after the magazine accepts the article for publication. "On publication" means the magazine will pay the author after the article has been published, which may be several months or even a year after acceptance. (See also Kill Fee.)

Query Generally, a one-page letter a freelance writer sends to a magazine editor outlining a proposed article and offering background information about the writer.

Rights The terms upon which a magazine acquires from an author the right to publish the author's copyrighted work. There are four basic rights:

- **All rights** means the magazine has, in fact, purchased the copyright from the author and can, therefore, publish the author's work at any time and in any fashion. The author no longer has any right to the article. A similar term is **Work for Hire.** More and more publishers are purchasing all rights to avoid negotiating with authors over additional pay if the author's work is used in more than one medium.

- **Electronic Rights** CD-ROM and the Internet have changed the magazine industry. For example, should a publisher pay an author additional fees if the publisher places the article in three different formats? Established authors, in particular, may negotiate fees based on what uses the publisher plans to make of the author's work.

- **First Serial Rights** means the magazine purchases the exclusive right to publish an article for the first time.

- **One Time Rights** means the magazine may print the article, but not exclusively. The article also could be published at the same time by other, noncompeting publications.

SASE Self-addressed stamped envelope. What an author includes with a query letter.

Sidebar A short article that accompanies and complements a longer feature.

Specialization A category of magazines whose content and audience are narrowly focused. For example, women's magazines.

Speculation An author may submit an article to a magazine on speculation. That means the publisher can reject the article and pay nothing.

Writer's Guidelines A set of how-to instructions and recommendations prepared by a magazine to advise writers how to prepare and submit articles for that publication. They are usually sent free to an author upon request (and a SASE).

APPENDIX B

Resources

We have listed a number of resources that can be helpful to you as a writer for magazines. Some you may already be aware of, but others may be new to you. The list includes both print and online resources. This is by no means a complete or exclusive list of all resources a writer may need or wish to consult in the course of researching and composing an article. Since the subjects of magazine articles and the interests of writers are so widely varied, no such list is possible.

American Business Media: This organization in New York City is a good source of information about business-to-business/trade publications in the United States. Contact at www.americanbusinesspress.com or call the manager of information services at (212) 661-6360, ext. 3329.

Bacon's Magazine Directory: The Directory lists more than 30,000 consumer and trade publications, organized by categories. Information supplied for each magazine listed includes the following: publication profile; address, phone, and fax numbers; e-mail address; circulation, and key editors. The Directory is published annually and may be purchased from Bacon's Information Inc. in Chicago, but it is expensive. You would do better to consult the Directory in your college library or, possibly, in the journalism department.

The Elements of Style: This thin, little book by William Strunk Jr. and E. B. White has helped several generations of writers improve their writing big time. It can help you, too, through such chapters as Elementary Principles of Composition, Words and Expressions Commonly Misused, and An Approach to Style. Available in book stores and libraries.

Encyclopedia of Associations: This directory lists nearly all professional associations in America. Each association's listing includes information about magazines and newsletters published by the association. The directory provides another, perhaps even more important service for the writer. No matter what subject an author is writing about, it probably is the primary concern of some association. Writing about the effect on traffic flow of new, automated toll collecting systems? Contact the International Municipal Signal Association. Writing about what really happens in hospital emergency rooms? Contact the American College of Emergency Physicians.

Error-Free Writing: This paperback by Robin A. Cormier, subtitled A Lifetime Guide to Flawless Business Writing, offers a number of good tips on writing and rewriting, but it is especially helpful for two appendices. One is an excellent list of standard abbreviations; the other is a guide to compound words that indicates what ones are hyphenated and what ones are not. Available in book stores and some libraries. Also, may be purchased from Prentice-Hall, Englewood Cliffs, NJ.

E-zine Directory. The official title is The Free Directory of E-zines. The Directory can be found at www.freezineweb.com.

Folio: The Magazine for Magazine Management: This publication about the industry is published 17 times a year and covers trends and issues affecting magazines (and, often, writers). The print version is available in many libraries; the online version, which has links to past editions, is found at www.foliomag.com.

Magazines for Kids and Teens: A directory of some 200 magazines published exclusively for children aged one to 18 arranged alphabetically by age group and by subject matter. Many of the publications are not found in other directories. Each listing provides information about the magazine and its audience, name of editor, address and phone number. The directory is published by Association of Educational Publishers and may be purchased from that organization at 510 Heron Dr., Suite 309, Logan Township, NJ 08085. It also may be found in libraries.

Writer's Market: The annual directory of more than 1,700 consumer and trade magazines listed alphabetically within categories (for example, health and fitness and in-flight). Each listing supplies a wealth of information about the publication and its audience, kinds of articles it is in the market for, tips to freelancers from editors, name and address of editors, and more. Available in book stores and libraries.

Writer On Line: This is a free online service available at www.novalearn.com. Each edition includes information about the magazine marketplace and about various products and services for writers.

writersweekly.com: This is an excellent and free online newsletter that may be the best source available of up-to-date listings of paying markets for freelancers. Each edition also includes information about e-books for writers and writing and questions and answers concerning trends and issues affecting writers.

APPENDIX C

Optional Classroom Activities

All suggested activities should be undertaken only with the approval and at the direction of the teacher. Some of the activities listed below may have been suggested in Hands On sections of various chapters but are further developed and explained here.

Magazine Analysis

All editors plead with writers to study their magazine before querying as a freelancer or, for that matter, before applying for a staff position. Early classroom activities may include analyzing consumer and trade magazines in groups of two or three students. Each group may examine one, two, or three magazines. Students identify audience demographics based on article content and advertisements, look for organizational formulas and patterns, and note differences and similarities in writing style. The same groups also may determine how many articles are written by freelancers, and students can get a feel for staff size and positions by consulting magazine mastheads. Magazines selected for analysis may include some well known to students, but an effort should be made to include publications that are unfamiliar to most students.

Testing Ideas

After students select one or more ideas they consider worthy subjects for an article, they meet in small groups of two or three to test out their idea(s) with classmates. The critique should be constructive, but honest and blunt.

Interview Demonstration

The interview is often the most critical step in the research process. It also is the step that many students find difficult, even intimidating. Classroom practice in interviewing may be helpful. Here are three different ways to demonstrate the interview process.

First, select an interesting person from on or off campus whose knowledge and/or experience could legitimately qualify as ingredients for a magazine article. Brief the interviewee as follows: He/she will be the subject of interview for a magazine article; he/she should answer questions fully, but not volunteer information not asked for even if that information might be important or enlightening.

Brief all students on the background of the interviewee and why that person's knowledge and/or experience might be worthy of a magazine article. Instruct all students to prepare questions in advance of the scheduled interview.

At the time of the interview, select one student to ask questions. The student interviewee has a set time for the interview, perhaps 15 minutes. At the end of the interview, all students, teacher, and interviewee critique the interview. Was the interviewer well prepared? Was the interviewee responsive? Was valuable time wasted with some unnecessary and unfruitful discussion? What questions were not asked that should have been? Were follow-up opportunities missed?

In a small class—10–15 students—students may take turns asking questions of the interviewee.

Students choose a person to interview from a list of preselected candidates whose knowledge and/or experience could be a basis for a magazine article (trade or consumer). The number of candidates equal the number of students. Students are arbitrarily assigned a candidate, or each student draws the name of a candidate to be interviewed.

Again, candidates are briefed. Students have a deadline to arrange for the interview, prepare questions, and conduct the interview. As part of an in-class activity, students meet in groups of two or three prior to interviews and critique each other's approach to the topic and prepared questions.

To conclude any of the three demonstrations, students write a one- or two-page paper stating the following:

- How they could use the results of the interview to develop a magazine article. Direct quotation and paraphrase should be cited.
- What prepared questions proved most valuable and most unhelpful.
- In retrospect, what additional questions should have been asked?
- If the interviewee opened up an interesting area for discussion not anticipated, was the opportunity seized upon?
- What additional research (including other interviews) might be needed if a magazine article based on the interview is written?

These papers could be discussed in small groups and/or collected by the teacher for evaluation and discussion with individual students.

Critiquing Queries

After students have drafted query letters to editors, they meet with one other student and exchange query letters. Students should be prepared to react as an editor might. Questions they might ask are these:

- Given the subject matter of the proposed article, is the letter directed at the right publication and audience?
- Does the lead grab attention and make the topic interesting? Is enough helpful information about the proposed article supplied?
- Has the author given sufficient and pertinent biographical information on himself/herself?

Talking With Writers

Writers learn from other writers—and editors. Students benefit from talking with a successful freelance writer, an established magazine staff writer, and a magazine editor whose duties include reviewing queries and assigning articles. These three persons are invited to speak to the class on separate occasions. It is helpful if they talk not only about their present work but also about their college and other experiences that prepared them for current responsibilities.

Reading Articles

When students feel confident their articles are ready for submission to a magazine, they are invited to read their article before classmates. This is an excellent culminating activity, especially if students have previously critiqued each other's article ideas and query letters. Now they discover how early efforts panned out.

INDEX